Relax

Quadrille

Relax – it's only food

John Torode with **Sheila Keating**

Photography by David Loftus

To Angie. Marcel and Casper

First published in 1999 by
Quadrille Publishing Limited,
Alhambra House,
27–31 Charing Cross Road,
London WC2H OLS

ISBN 1 902757 16 5

Publishing Director: Anne Furniss
Creative Director: Mary Evans
Project Editor: Lewis Esson
Design: Lawrence Morton
Photography: David Loftus
Illustrations: Bruce Ingman
Production: Julie Hadingham

Printed and bound in Singapore by
KHL. Printing Co Pte Ltd
Colour separations by Colourscan,
Singapore

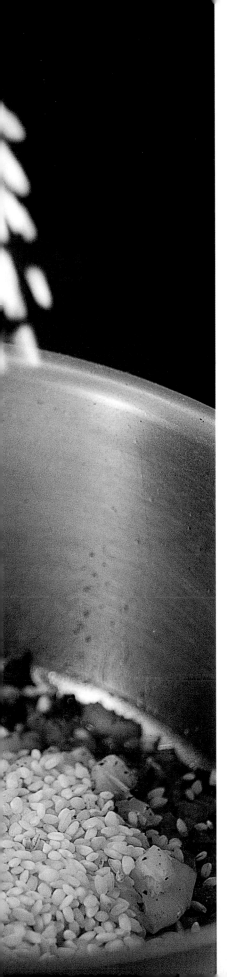

Contents

Recipes

> **❛Great food is whatever fits the mood of the moment❜**

On this list and throughout the book, recipes that don't actually appear under their own heading but are woven into the narrative text are indicated by asterisks*.

Throughout the book recipes are for four people unless otherwise stated.

Introduction

'The food I get excited about isn't fussed around with; it is simple and tasty, and all bound up with feelings and memories of people and places'

I have had some of my best times cooking with family and friends, sharing food that isn't pretentious or expensive or particularly serious. I love that relaxed way of preparing meals where one person opens a bottle of wine, another cuts up bread or dresses a salad, you turn up the music and everyone is chatting and enjoying themselves.

The food I get excited about isn't fussed around with; it is simple and tasty, and all bound up with feelings and memories of people and places. Great food is whatever fits the mood of the moment: I will always remember char-grilled red mullet with tapenade and rocket leaves at a pavement table in the sunshine outside a bistro in Nice, hours before flying home from a fantastic holiday. Then on a trip to Thailand I was overwhelmed by the generosity of families in mountain villages who had little more than some vegetables, chillies and galangal, herbs and sticky rice, but wanted to share them. The fiery flavoursome meals that came out of those simple ingredients were quite amazing.

I think of crazy barbecues in our garden in north London, roasting whole pieces of veal with shallots, and winter evenings after school at my grandmother's house in Maitland in Australia, tucking into grilled lamb chops with their edge of fat mouthwateringly crispy and caramelized, and mashed potato, with rhubarb cooked in a slow oven to follow. Later Christmases in Australia, when we would put a whole cooked ham in a pillowcase in the fridge so that on Christmas morning we could crack open a bottle of Champagne, and cut the ham into thick slices and have it on wedges of buttery toast.

I'll take those meals and memories any day over a stilted dinner party where the cook is trying to impress with fiddled-around-with-food, with ten sauces and as many flavours all fighting for attention. Why agonize and worry about complicated dishes when you could boil a chicken and put it in the middle of the table with some garlicky mayonnaise, a big dish of potatoes, a bowl of salad and maybe some sausages on the side for the kids, then let everyone get involved with the food, picking up bits of chicken, using their fingers? Sometimes I think we get too anxious and precious by half about cooking, and maybe the recent popularity of chefs and cooking programmes has to take the blame for some of that. In this book, though, you won't find any references to things like chiffonnade and julienne and tomato concassé.

As far as I'm concerned if you have to blanch, skin, deseed and chop a tomato before you can put it on a plate, then it's no good; throw it in the bin. In one kitchen, where I worked when I was training, we were supposed to make tomato soup with 10 kilos of peeled, deseeded and chopped tomatoes, which then got put in a pot and boiled up for about 4½ hours. So where were all those little cubes of tomatoes, then? If you don't want seeds and skin in a soup or sauce, sieve them out at the end of cooking, I say.

Like most people, I suspect, I cook according to the way I feel. What do I fancy eating? Something spicy, something comforting, something light, or a bit posh, or a really classical dish like a Caesar salad that I have made over and over again, but will never bore me? That is why I have divided the book up according to different moods. Occasionally I just get a craving for something really naughty, like custard from a carton or thousand island dressing with a piece of crisp lettuce wrapped around it. Well, as far as I'm concerned, that's OK too. I'm not interested in snobbery in food, or food as fashion, or one-upmanship. I'm just interested in great food.

To me the dish of spaghetti with prawns and macadamia nuts that I used to cook as an apprentice in Australia years ago was good food then, and it still is, and I'll carry on making it for as long as I feel that way — just as I would love to think that in twenty years' time someone might still pick

'I'm not interested in snobbery in food, or food as fashion, or one-upmanship. I'm just interested in great food'

up this book and make great fishcakes. Equally I get excited by new flavours and ideas and techniques; by Japanese food and Indonesian food or by something I've seen in a café or a market while on holiday.

Mostly, though, I just get excited about ingredients. Forget glamorous kitchen gadgets, you can get by on a big knife and a little knife, a big pot and a little pot, as long as you have great ingredients. Often when I am shopping for food for dinner with half an idea in my head, I will throw it out completely and decide to cook something entirely different, because I have seen a fabulous turbot or a gorgeous piece of marbled beef, or a box of great aubergines. Even when I am reading or watching a movie, my mind is never far away from food, which drives my wife Angie crazy sometimes, but I've always been the same.

I pick up one of my kids' books on dinosaurs, and I'm making comparisons between their eggs and hens' eggs; I read *Moby Dick*, and the thing that stays with me is the chowder houses, where the people ate it for breakfast, lunch and tea. Three types, all sounding delicious: cod or clam, with bacon and potatoes, and a big one made with cod and clams. In my mind I can pick up a spoonful of that chowder and put it in my mouth and enjoy those flavours. I just love cooking, and handling food and tasting it and I get excited even talking about it, not because it is high art, but because it is fun.

This isn't meant to be a textbook, just a collection of ideas that I hope will inspire you to play about with the recipes as you like, and above all to relax and enjoy cooking and eating for what it should be: a pleasure and a delight, not something deadly serious, or snobbish or stressful. Because when all is said and done, it is only food…

> 'I just love cooking, and handling food and tasting it and I get excited even talking about it, not because it is high art, but because it is fun'

John Torode

Light

I have a quintessential midsummer memory of a day during a holiday with my wife, Angie, and some friends in the south of France, when we crossed by boat to St Tropez market, one of the most extraordinary markets I have ever been to. The place seemed to be full of beautiful women dressed in white who'd just stepped off their yachts, looking like they'd never been shopping for food before, walking through the old streets, carrying big bunches of flowers in their arms, captivated by the stalls piled high with gorgeous cheeses, sausages, big bunches of herbs and fresh fish.

We bought parcels of roast pork from the rôtisserie, *saucisson*, slabs of cheese and pâté, bags of big ripe tomatoes and armfuls of bread, then climbed up the side of the hill overlooking the harbour and put down someone's shirt for a cloth, opened up a couple of bottles of wine with Angie's trusty penknife and had a fantastic lunch. Then we all fell asleep in the sun!

Light food doesn't have to be associated with summer – but somehow in my mind it usually is. At the first hint of sunshine I want to fire up the barbie and lay tables in the garden, and go shopping in that relaxed, browsing way that you do on holiday – with no real recipes in mind, just buying ingredients because you can't resist them – the irony being that you invariably buy so much 'light' food you have to invite the neighbours around... but that's all part of the fun.

I grew up with the Australian lifestyle of being in and out of everyone else's backyards all summer. On holidays at my aunt's house in New South Wales, the barbie always seemed to be going. Someone would drive out to the estuary at Hexham, where the prawn trucks parked, and buy a couple of kilos of big red prawns wrapped in paper, and a tub of Marie Rose sauce with extra Tabasco.

> **Light food doesn't have to be associated with summer – but somehow in my mind it usually is**

11

Light

Someone else would turn up with containers of salad, or a pavlova laden with passion fruit, or a crate of beer. We'd peel the prawns – throwing the shells into a bowl as if we were eating peanuts – squeeze lemons over them and dip them into the sauce, while we waited for the steaks to finish cooking on the barbie, or fresh fish, which you could break into sweetly charred chunks and spear on forks to dip into jars of mayonnaise.

What that first visit to the south of France did for me was change my whole opinion about food outside Australia. When I was growing up, we had always seen French food as a pretentious, complicated art form, but now I was totally seduced by the way the people spent their mornings at the market, hopping from stall to stall in search of the best produce for a simple lunch or dinner.

Everything about that trip is heightened in my memory: the day fishing boats coming into the harbour selling John Dory at extortionate prices, and the burnt mountain landscape near where we stayed at St Maxime, where the ground had been torched by the locals to improve the conditions for the next year's crop of morel mushrooms. Over long lunch times, extended families sat out on their verandas, around tables laden with food and bottles of wine, and in the evenings the local lads played table football in the bars, while the women sat chatting on benches and the men played *boules*.

I remember joining the queue outside the butchers, which meant sitting outside in the sun, chatting with the other customers for half an hour before we were served, then being mesmerized by the skill of the butcher, slowly and carefully scoring and dressing our leg of lamb ready for the barbecue. Light food for me is a reflection of that wonderful slow pace of holiday eating, and the lifestyle I knew in Australia. I think of light food as totally relaxed, and mostly unconstructed. It is about bowlfuls of simple dishes that everyone can dip into and share, or layer up between slabs of crusty bread. It's a great chance to do what other cultures do in warm countries... graze. Think of the Thais, who typically eat bowlfuls of small dishes six or seven times a day, the Greeks with their *meze*, the Spanish with *tapas*.

Light food is a mix of things you make and things you buy, like Parma ham or chorizo or *falafel* made with chickpea flour (originally it was broad bean flour), crunchy on the outside and soft inside; or chunks of haloumi cheese, threaded on skewers with mushrooms and toasted on the barbecue, until the cheese is golden and chewy and salty.

I guess my notion of light food is as much a state of mind as anything else. On a miserable day, when I'm feeling homesick for the beach and sunshine, I can turn up the heating, buy a crispy-skinned chicken from the local rôtisserie, make a bunch of salads, chill some beers, spread the lot out on the table and change the mood. It's my take on what they used to do in a famous pub called the Albury in Sydney. During winter they would throw sand all over the floor and get out the beach balls, then everyone would strip off their winter woollies and party.

What I am trying to do in this chapter is to give a succession of ideas that I

❝ I think of light food as totally relaxed, and mostly unconstructed. It is about bowlfuls of simple dishes that everyone can dip into and share ❞

associate with light, summery food. You can make the whole lot and throw a party or just do one thing, because light food – like comfort food – is often about that single, simple dish that completely satisfies your needs at a specific moment. I remember arriving in Rome with a group of chefs very late one night. In a piazza we found a restaurant that was still open and asked what they had that was good. We'd just got off a plane and didn't want much to eat, just something tasty and a chance to relax over a glass of wine and some decent conversation. The waiter said he could bring some *fettuccine* with fresh *porcini*, and when the bowls of fresh ribbon pasta arrived, tossed through with beautiful, thickly sliced mushrooms and parsley and olive oil and fresh parmesan, we sat in that square in that beautiful city in the warmth of the night, thinking, 'This is as good as it gets.'

Fish Whole fish or fillets, or sweet scallops, roasted over twigs of rosemary or thyme, until they are charred and caramelized and sweet around the edges, encapsulate the idea of simple light food for me.

I love tuna steaks, cut thick as fillet steak, smeared in a little olive oil, seasoned with salt and freshly ground pepper, and char-grilled really quickly (3 or 4 minutes on each side), so that they are nice and rare on the inside. Just squeeze a lemon over the top and away you go. You can cook swordfish steaks in the same way.

Barbecued sardines are another favourite, though as a child I hated sardines because I only ever had them out of a tin. I remember my grandmother loved tinned sardines on toast, and the smell of them would linger throughout her house. Then, one summer in Portugal, I ate a plate of fresh sardines in a bar clinging to the side of a rock overlooking the beach, where the menu was written on a blackboard and a couple of guys barbecued the fish on grills set on top of oil drums filled with coals. Those sardines, with just a basket of bread and a bottle of cheap chilled rosé wine, altered my opinion of these marvellous oily little fish for ever.

After that I kept going to buy them from the vast local fish market, with its beautiful fish-patterned mosaic floors and marble slabs piled with huge purple or orange prawns, great tuna and mullet and swordfish. At the clam stall you could hear the little molluscs all hissing away – cherrystones, razors, *palourdes*. And there was fantastic squid, which you could score with a sharp knife, dip briefly in olive oil and sear on the barbecue, then serve it on some lettuce leaves with a dressing of chopped chillies and lime juice.

I usually make ✳ **Barbecued Sardines in Vine Leaves**. For 10 cleaned and gutted sardines, I mix up a stuffing made from a small bunch each of coriander and mint, chopped up with a crushed clove or two of garlic, 50 g of pine nuts dry-roasted in a hot pan until they change colour then chopped, 50 g raisins soaked for an hour or two in some Earl Grey tea then chopped, and the peel from a Preserved Lemon (see page 23) cut into strips. I stuff the mixture into the cavities of the sardines, wrap them in the vine leaves, then barbecue or grill them for about 3 minutes on each side (you can also use sardine fillets, rolled up around the stuffing and wrapped in the leaves in the same way). When the sardines are ready, unwrap them and drizzle over some extra-virgin olive oil and a little lemon juice, then sprinkle with salt.

> **At the clam stall you could hear the little molluscs all hissing away – cherrystones, razors, *palourdes***

Red Mullet with Chard, Lemon and Capers

I like to cook fish like red mullet whole, as it stays nice and moist on the bone, whereas the fillets will dry out quickly.

If you are cooking whole fish like this, try to get your fishmonger to snip the gills and draw the gut out through them, as the Chinese usually do, so the belly doesn't have to be slit and you can then keep all the flavour inside the fish.

200 g chard, leaves and stalks
   separated
salt
4 whole red mullet, each about 200 g,
   cleaned and gutted (or 8 fillets)
a little olive oil
50 g butter
juice of 1 lemon
handful of salted capers, rinsed
handful of roughly chopped parsley

1 Light the barbecue or preheat a hot grill. Blanch the chard stalks briefly in boiling salted water for a few minutes until they are almost soft, then add the leaves and cook both together for a minute or so longer, until both leaves and stalks are just tender. Drain them well.

2 Rub the mullet with a little olive oil and cook on the barbecue or under the hot grill for about 5–6 minutes on each side (allow slightly less time for fillets if you are using them) and let the fish rest briefly in a warm place before serving.

3 While the fish is cooking, heat the butter in a pan, add the drained chard stalks and leaves and stir around until they are heated through. Let the butter turn brown, then add the lemon juice and rinsed capers and serve with the fish, sprinkled liberally with some chopped parsley.

Red mullet fillets cooked in this way can also be served as an ✳ **Escabèche**: grilled fish, marinated in vinegar and herbs. To make a marinade for 8 fillets, heat a little olive oil in a pan and add a thinly sliced carrot, a couple of chopped shallots and a sliced garlic clove. Sprinkle in some thyme leaves and then add 100 ml white wine vinegar, 5 tablespoons of water, a tablespoon of lemon juice and a few threads of saffron, first heated in a dry pan to release their aroma. Then leave the mixture to cool. When the grilled fish have cooled, put them in a non-reactive bowl, pour the marinade over the top and leave overnight in the fridge before serving.

Sea Bass with Ginger and Spring Onion

This is the traditional Chinese way of steaming whole fish, but if you want to cook it out of doors, you could just as easily wrap it in banana leaves, if you have them, or baking paper, then in a layer of foil, and put the parcel on the barbecue. Unwrap the fish and finish it off with hot oil and spring onions in the same way.

Serves around 4

banana leaves (optional)
1 sea bass, about 900 g, preferably
   gutted through the gills (see opposite)
25 g fresh ginger, cut into thin strips
4 spring onions, sliced at an angle
2 tablespoons Shaoxing wine (Chinese
   rice wine)
1 tablespoon light soy sauce
about 4 teaspoons groundnut or
   sesame oil

1 Put a suitable plate inside a steamer, preferably bamboo, and line with banana leaves if you have them. Lay the fish on top and sprinkle over the ginger and half the spring onions. Mix together the rice wine, soy sauce and about 3 tablespoons of water. Pour over the fish.

2 Steam the fish for 12 minutes, then remove from the heat.
3 In a small pan, heat the groundnut or sesame oil until it is beginning to smoke. Scatter the rest of the spring onions over the sea bass and pour over the hot oil, so that it sizzles.

Barbecued Lamb

A leg of lamb roasted on a barbecue in Corsica or on a beach in Greece, or in your garden with friends on a hot day, tastes totally different from a leg of lamb roasted in the oven on a rainy Sunday in North London, partly because we treat it differently. In winter I want to serve lamb with roast potatoes and vegetables and good gravy, but in summer a leg of lamb speaks to me of clay ovens or coals, of marinades made with yoghurt, lemon juice and herbs and spices, and side dishes of spicy aubergine *baba ganoush* or *imam bayildi*, and *tabbouleh* – bulgar wheat with masses of mint and parsley and lemon juice.

One of my favourite dishes is ✳ **Barbecued Lamb Marinated in Yoghurt**. You first need to tenderize the lamb by rubbing it with a mixture of the juice of 2 lemons, a tablespoon of salt and a handful of thyme leaves, then leave it for a few hours. Then you need around 250 ml yoghurt, to which you add a paste made by blitzing in a food processor 2 deseeded and chopped red chillies, a handful of chopped coriander, 2 chopped garlic cloves, a pinch of salt and some freshly ground black pepper, together with 1 tablespoon of cinnamon and half a tablespoon each of cardamom, cloves and turmeric, all dry-roasted in a pan (alternatively you could flavour the yoghurt with some ground cumin or garam masala, first roasted briefly in a dry pan to release their aroma). Rub the marinade into the lamb all over.

Leave overnight before barbecuing with some big sprigs of rosemary, preferably straight from the garden, so that it has that beautiful oily freshness that is often lost in the thin, lavender-smelling – usually forced – herb packaged for supermarkets. If you haven't got any in the garden, take a walk around your neighbourhood with a pair of scissors, because someone is bound to have some in the front garden and will let you have a little if you ask nicely. If you plant some young shoots straight in the ground or a pot on a windowsill, a number of them will take in spring.

Barbecue the lamb for about 30 minutes for quite pink meat, then finish with lemon juice and leave it to rest for about 10 minutes before slicing it. Serve it with chunks of Greek-style flat bread and ✳ **Tzatziki** – yoghurt mixed with sliced cucumber, some chopped mint, a pinch of salt and a good squeeze of lemon juice. You could also barbecue some Greek or Cypriot lamb sausages – really dense, full of cumin and paprika and garlic – or *merguez*, or put out some cured chorizo. I love sausages, in any shape or form. I think they are God's own food.

Light

Imam Bayildi The Turkish *imam bayildi*, which translates as 'the priest fainted', is a fantastic dish, made with aubergines and spices, and traditionally served with lamb. There are two stories about how it got its name. The first is that when the priest's wife made this new dish for him, it was so delicious that he fainted with delight; the other is that it was so packed with rich and expensive ingredients, like dried fruit, olive oil and aubergines, that when the plate arrived in front of him he fainted at the cost!

There are two problems that can spoil the dish: it can be dry if you don't fry the spices in a good amount of oil, and it can be over-greasy if you use too much oil when you fry the aubergines. Because raw aubergines absorb so much oil, I do as the Chinese do and steam or boil them before frying.

Serves 4–6 with other dishes

3 aubergines
1 teaspoon ground turmeric
2 teaspoons cumin seeds
1 teaspoon coriander seeds
1 cardamom pod
150 ml olive oil
3 garlic cloves, roughly chopped
3 very ripe plum tomatoes, chopped
1 tablespoon sultanas
good handful of chopped flat-leaf parsley

1 Cut the aubergine into cubes of about 3 cm and steam or boil in salted water until just soft. Drain well.
2 Grind the whole spices (alternatively use ground spices).

3 Heat the olive oil in a heavy-based pan, add the spices and cook for a few minutes until you have an aromatic paste.
4 Add the chunks of aubergine and the chopped garlic. Stir everything around, then let the mixture sit for a few minutes over the heat until it colours nicely on the underside. Turn the mixture over and leave until the other side colours in the same way.
5 Add the tomatoes, stir briefly and take the pan off the heat. Stir in the sultanas and leave to cool, then mix in the chopped parsley.
6 Leave for about 6 hours before serving, so that the flavours can really infuse the aubergines.

The other big-flavoured aubergine dish that is great with lamb or other barbecued meat (but not pork, which doesn't go with the smoky oiliness of the aubergine) is ✳**Baba Ganoush**. It also works well with food like scallops, or a piece of charred salmon. I really like to get a smoky aubergine flavour, so I put the whole aubergine either on the barbecue or on a fork over a gas flame until the skin blisters and chars and starts to break apart and the flesh inside is really soft. If you don't have gas, then put the aubergine into an oven preheated as high as you can get it. When the aubergine is ready, I scrape off the outside of the skin, but leave that smoky dark layer beneath, which adds so much flavour. For 2 aubergines, you also need to chop 2 garlic cloves and roast a teaspoon each of cumin and coriander seeds in a dry pan until they colour and release their aroma, then grind them. Put them into a food processor with the aubergine, 150 g tahini (sesame paste), a teaspoon of salt, the juice of 1 lemon, 150 ml extra-virgin olive oil and 3 tablespoons water, then purée the whole thing until it changes from purply-brown to almost white. Taste and season if necessary; you might also want to add a little more lemon juice.

Tabbouleh

Serves 6–8 with other dishes

250 g fine-ground bulgar wheat
100 ml extra-virgin olive oil
juice of 3 lemons
5 ripe tomatoes, finely chopped
3–4 spring onions, thinly sliced
good handful of flat-leaf parsley,
   chopped
good handful of mint leaves,
   chopped
salt and freshly ground black pepper

1 Soak the bulgar wheat in cold water for 30 minutes.
2 Drain well, pressing out excess water. In a bowl, mix thoroughly with half the olive oil and half the lemon juice. Leave about half an hour, to let the wheat soften a little more and absorb the flavours.
3 Just before serving, stir in the rest of the olive oil and lemon juice, with the remaining ingredients. If the mixture is too dry, add a little more oil. It should be quite sharp and fresh-tasting, so you may want to add more lemon juice.

On Toast

I reckon one definition of good food is that you can put it in a sandwich or pile it on toast or ✳ **Crostini** – slices of baguette or Italian country bread cut at an angle and put into an oven preheated to about 200°C/400°F/gas 6 for about 10 minutes until light gold and crisp, then rubbed with garlic and olive oil. I like to make bowls of spicy vegetable purées, like garlicky cauliflower, which is fantastic on a wedge of *crostini* topped with a slice of barbecued meat and some salad.

To make a bowlful of ✳ **Cauliflower Purée** for dipping, put half a medium cauliflower, broken into pieces, into a saucepan with a diced onion and 2 chopped garlic cloves, a pinch of salt and about 3 cm of water at the most. Cover with the lid and cook for about 10 minutes, until the water has evaporated and the cauliflower is soft. While the cauliflower is cooking, toast a teaspoonful of ground cumin in a dry pan to release its flavour, then add it to the cauliflower with a teaspoon of olive oil and continue to cook, moving the cauliflower around the pan as it begins to colour and caramelize. Add a few spoonfuls of water a little at a time, scraping the base of the pan to incorporate all the sweet bits of caramelized vegetable. Taste it and the cauliflower will be quite sweet. Mash the whole thing with a fork, or blitz briefly with a hand blender; add a little more olive oil if you want to loosen the texture a bit. Season with black pepper and a squeeze of lemon juice, and leave to cool.

You can make a similar ✳ **Garlic Purée** with just whole heads of garlic. Put them into a pan of water, bring it to the boil, then turn the heat down and simmer for 3–4 minutes. The boiling takes the acidic edge off the garlic. Leave until they are cool to the touch, then cut off the bases and pop the cloves out of their skins. Put them back into the pan, this time with just enough water to cover, a tablespoon of olive oil and a pinch of salt. Cover and cook until the water has evaporated and the garlic begins to hiss and sizzle (about 10 minutes). If you put a knife into the cloves they should be soft like butter. Blitz with a hand blender, adding a little more olive oil, until the purée is smooth, then allow to cool completely. Served on pieces of *crostini*, the effect is a bit like garlic bread with texture.

> **❝ I reckon one definition of good food is that you can put it in a sandwich or pile it on toast ❞**

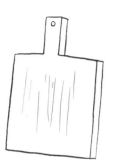

Anchovies on Toast

These are great on Crostini – or just a piece of toast – for a light lunch

Serves 2

200 g fresh anchovies
freshly ground black pepper
1 tablespoon white wine vinegar
2 tablespoons olive oil
juice and finely chopped zest of 1 lemon
handful of chopped flat-leaf parsley

The day before:
1 Season the anchovies with pepper and put into a non-reactive bowl.

2 Put the white wine vinegar into a small pan with a tablespoon of water and bring to the boil, remove the pan from the heat and stir in the olive oil and the lemon juice. Leave the mixture to cool.
3 Sprinkle the lemon zest over the anchovies and pour the cooled liquid over the top.
4 Cover and put in the fridge to marinate overnight.

Next day:
5 Serve on toast or Crostini, with the chopped parsley scattered liberally over the top.

Crostini are great topped with vegetables that have been marinated in garlic and olive oil before being cooked under a preheated hot grill or on the barbecue: try fennel slices, peppers or aubergines. Finish them off with a squeeze of lemon juice, lay them on the *crostini*, and scatter them with herbs and curls of parmesan, or a spoonful of tapenade.

To make a good bowlful of ✳**Tapenade** you need around 250 g pitted black olives and 40 g large salted capers, rinsed and dried. Using a pestle and mortar or food processor, crush half of each with a garlic clove and a tablespoon of olive oil, then add the rest of the olives and capers and 25 g rinsed salted anchovy fillets, and grind to a paste. At the last minute, add a tablespoon of brandy. Season as necessary and fold in some roughly chopped flat-leaf parsley.

If you have the time, you could make ✳**Marinated Aubergine Crostini**: grill or barbecue 2 or 3 aubergines cut into thick slices (about 1.5 cm), brush lightly in oil, then leave to cool. Make up your marinade with about 100 ml olive oil, a couple of chopped garlic cloves, a handful of chopped flat-leaf parsley, the juice and grated zest of 1 lemon and some salt and freshly ground black pepper. Pour some of the marinade into a non-reactive bowl, put in a layer of aubergine, then a little more marinade, more aubergine, etc., layering until you have used up all the aubergine. Pour the remaining marinade over the top and leave for 2–3 hours or overnight. Serve it on *crostini* with more olive oil if you like, and plenty of ground black pepper.

Or you could make ✳**Caponata**, with a couple of diced aubergines, fried in olive oil until brown and tender, then set aside while you cook a diced onion and a chopped tomato, seasoned well, in a little olive oil in a separate pan for about 15 minutes. Mix in a tablespoon of rinsed salted capers, a couple of chopped celery stalks, a handful of stoned green olives, 4 tablespoons of red wine vinegar and a

Light

tablespoon of sugar. Simmer for about 15 minutes, until the liquid reduces a little, stirring occasionally, then mix in the aubergine and leave to stand for at least half an hour before serving. I love caponata with thinly sliced Parma ham.

When I serve *crostini* with vegetables and hams and grilled fish, I always put out bottles of good olive oil, so that people can drizzle some more over the top: maybe a mixture of quite yellow Sicilian oil and the deeper green, grassy, peppery stuff that comes from Puglia and further north towards Tuscany, where the olive leaves are often added to enhance the stunning colour and distinctive flavour.

One ingredient that always feels summery, but isn't, is new-season's olive oil, which is actually available only from November to March. Sadly it's hard to get now, because so many olive oil producers are blending oils for supermarkets, and very few estate-bottled concerns are releasing new-season's oil, which is quite sharp and hot and potent, with slightly weird flavours like green bananas. If you can find it, buy it in small bottles and use it as quickly as you can, since it completely changes its character after only a few months. It is best raw, drizzled over *crostini* or grilled vegetables or mushrooms or a bowl of pasta, such as *pappardelle*.

✳ **Pappardelle with New-season's Olive Oil and Fennel** is a great light one-bowl dish. I slice the fennel and cook it briefly in olive oil ('old-season'), then add a bay leaf, a couple of star anise, season well and put in just enough water to cover. Then I simmer it in a big pan for about 2–3 minutes until just tender. I cook the *pappardelle* separately in plenty of boiling salted water (in a ratio of 1 litre of water to 100 g pasta), drain it, then tip it into the pan of fennel, toss the whole thing through with some thin slices of feta cheese, and a mixture of stoned black and green olives. Just before serving, I pour in plenty of new-season's olive oil and scatter over a good handful of chopped flat-leaf parsley and chervil, together with a sprinkling of fennel seeds that have been toasted until they colour in a dry pan.

Pasta, like many ingredients, is pretty schizophrenic. In winter a big bowlful is great comfort food; in summer, it can be really light and refreshing, depending on what you run through it – like strips of roast vegetables, olives, fresh anchovies, or a good, textured pesto. I like all the individual flavours of the pine nuts, parmesan and basil to come through in a pesto, rather than have them amalgamate too much. You might as well make a good 500 ml of it, as you can use it for so many things: to spread on Crostini, to add to a salad dressing, or put a spoonful on top of a pissaladière (see page 34), or a tomato tart made with a disc of puff pastry, pricked with a fork, then spread with some passata (tomato pulp) and topped with some roast tomatoes (see pages 24–5) and baked in an oven preheated to its highest setting for 2–3 minutes, then turned down to 200°C/400°F/gas 6 for the tart to be cooked for another 15 minutes, until it is golden. Any pesto you don't need immediately can be stored in an airtight sterilized jar for up to a month.

To make the ✳ **Pesto**, start with 50 g basil leaves and 75 g flat parsley leaves in a food processor with 125 g pine nuts and 3 chopped garlic cloves. Process to a rough paste then, with the motor running at a medium speed, gradually add 500 ml extra-virgin olive oil until it all binds, then stir in 125 g grated parmesan and season.

Salads

I get pretty excited about good salads, perhaps because like many people I have this grim memory of salads in the '70s, when it was fashionable to be the proud owner of a big clear plastic bowl, with matching salad servers. You chopped an iceberg lettuce with a tomato and some cucumber and onion, chucked it all in the bowl and mixed the whole thing up with something that went by the generic term 'French dressing'... and that was your salad. Worse still was when people made up their salads in advance and put them in the fridge, so that by the time you came to eat, everything was limp and mushy.

I think a salad deserves as much respect as any other dish. You have to play around with textures: soft leaves against something with crunch and bite, like French beans, blanched very briefly so they are still crispy, then chopped; or young, raw broad beans; sliced shallots; or even some ✳ **Roast Rice** – basmati rice that's been soaked in water for 5 minutes, drained and then roasted for about half an hour in an oven preheated to 180°C/350°F/gas 4 until it turns off-white and releases a nutty aroma. I sometimes use rice instead of baking beans when I am baking pastry cases blind, then keep it in an airtight container for sprinkling into salads.

I think you also need something sweet against something sour. You don't have to use elaborate ingredients: the sweetness can come from a raw vegetable, a really ripe tomato or a roast onion; the sourness from vinegar or a squeeze of citrus fruit juice, or even a handful of olives. I also like a hit of something pure and strong, perhaps unexpected: it could be a chopped chilli, some slivers of rind from a preserved lemon (see below) or a handful of capers.

Finally you need a dressing, or even a significant herb, that draws all the different flavours and textures together. For a basic vinaigrette I usually use three parts good extra-virgin olive oil to one part red wine vinegar. To make a more unctuous dressing for coating, say, a tomato salad, I mix a little Dijon mustard with the vinegar before slowly whisking in the olive oil. When I add dressings to salads I always mix them with my hands, a little at a time, so that I can feel what is going on and stop when all the ingredients are bound together but not saturated. You need to taste as you go, and maybe add a little more oil or vinegar, or a squeeze of lemon juice, because the flavours of ingredients can change once they are dressed, and leaves that might have seemed pretty tasteless can soak up the dressing like sponges.

One of my favourite salads is made with roast tomatoes and the sliced peel of lemons preserved in salt, which are a major ingredient from North Africa to Israel. In France, where the North African influence is strong, ✳ **Preserved Lemons** are known as *citrons confits*. They can be used in all kinds of ways: with grilled meat or fish, and in North African-style *tajines* and stews. Preserved lemons, merguez and Harissa (see page 75) – now that's a great mix. Though recipes from different cultures vary, some involving spices and garlic, the basic idea stays the same: the salt acts on the lemon rind to soften it and intensify the flavour.

You need crystals of rock or sea salt, as refined table salt (which is mixed with magnesium carbonate) would just burn into the tomato and disappear. Rock salt is

Light

mined from dried-up lakes underground; sea salt is produced by the natural evaporation in the sunshine of the salt in the sea. I usually use Maldon sea salt from Essex, where the salt is extracted from the estuary water by dehydration and piled up in beautiful glistening mounds. It is lovely, pure stuff; if you run your fingers through the white crystals you will find that some still form perfect little pyramids.

Use unwaxed, preferably organic, lemons with thin skins and not too much pith, and scrub them really well. The traditional way of preparing them is to cut into each lemon at the pointed end and slice as if into quarters – but stop about 1 cm short of the base, so that the sections are held together. Then prise the segments open gently and push in about one teaspoon of sea salt. Close the lemons up again, pack them tightly into a sterilized jar, and weight them down – traditionally this would be done with a scrubbed and sterilized stone. This helps to press the juice out of the lemons and keep them underneath this liquid while they are maturing. If necessary the liquid can be topped up with more lemon juice. The jar is then sealed and stored for about 4 weeks until the lemons are ready. Then you use only the peel, cut into strips – discard the flesh as it tastes pretty awful.

I make my preserved lemons slightly differently in that I blanch them first for 10 seconds only in boiling water to which salt has been added in a ratio of 2 parts salt to 10 parts water. Then I cut them as above and pack them with salt. When the brine is cold, I use it to cover the lemons in the jar. Doing it this way keeps the vibrant colour of the lemons, otherwise they tend to turn a browny-yellow colour that is neither here nor there in a stew, but doesn't look so attractive in a salad. To a jarful of lemons I also add a small handful of star anise, a handful of coriander seeds and a couple of cinnamon sticks that have first been roasted in a dry pan until aromatic.

Roast Tomatoes When I was growing up in Australia, there must have been at least 30 or 40 huge glasshouses situated near our home. My brother and I used to help pick the tomatoes grown in them: rows upon rows. At first, the vine smell on your hands was wonderful, but after a few days it became gut-wrenching. You would end up with resin on your fingers and every time you moved them they would crack. Where have all those places gone? I sometimes wonder, and where has the flavour gone from most tomatoes? I guess it disappeared when producers started breeding bright-red, thick-skinned fruit that wouldn't bruise easily, as demanded by retailers.

When I was leaving Australia, the big fashion for sun-dried tomatoes was just starting to happen. I remember people being so disillusioned when they found out that they weren't ripened in the sun after all but in great tin aircraft hangers, with huge heaters that turned them into ovens, so the tomatoes would dry over a few days. I have always hated them; they make me think of caramel chewing gum. For me the half-dried tomatoes in this salad win every time over fruit that has been left to dry out completely. The idea is to cut some plum tomatoes in half, cover them with sea salt and herbs and put them in the oven on the lowest possible heat, until the tomatoes shrink to about half their size. Since you need only a gentle heat, you could also leave the tray of tomatoes above the stove when it is in use, over a radiator, or on a sunny windowsill in summer.

The process is all about osmosis. The herbs are crushed, rather than chopped, so that their oils seep out into the tomato, infusing it with a wonderful flavour, and at the same time the salt begins to draw out moisture. After a few hours the salt and herbs and tomato juices all form a lovely crust on the outside of the fruit, but the inside stays moist, so when you take a bite the sensation is a bit like eating a soft-centred chocolate.

I like to put a whole plate of roast tomatoes out at a barbecue, or use them in a bit of a play on the Italian classic of ✳ **Tomato and Mozzarella Salad**, with good buffalo mozzarella sliced quite thickly, combined with some beetroot, sorrel and rocket leaves, tossed with flat-leaved parsley and slices of shallot. You get a great combination of flavours from the sweetness of the beetroot, the sharpness of the sorrel and the peppery heat of the rocket. For the dressing, I purée about 30 g of sorrel to 125 ml of extra-virgin olive oil and season it with pepper and a dash of lemon juice. Sorrel is one of those herbs that should be used raw and quickly, as the flavour dies on you very swiftly. Also blanched or cooked sorrel has a certain quality which makes it indigestible for some people.

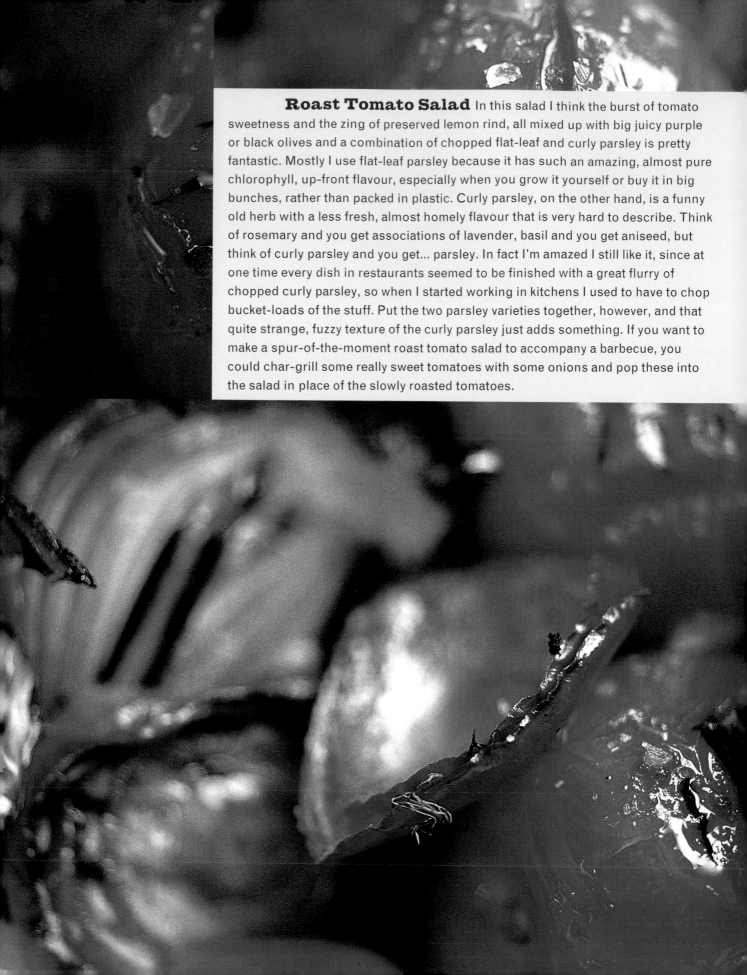

Roast Tomato Salad In this salad I think the burst of tomato sweetness and the zing of preserved lemon rind, all mixed up with big juicy purple or black olives and a combination of chopped flat-leaf and curly parsley is pretty fantastic. Mostly I use flat-leaf parsley because it has such an amazing, almost pure chlorophyll, up-front flavour, especially when you grow it yourself or buy it in big bunches, rather than packed in plastic. Curly parsley, on the other hand, is a funny old herb with a less fresh, almost homely flavour that is very hard to describe. Think of rosemary and you get associations of lavender, basil and you get aniseed, but think of curly parsley and you get... parsley. In fact I'm amazed I still like it, since at one time every dish in restaurants seemed to be finished with a great flurry of chopped curly parsley, so when I started working in kitchens I used to have to chop bucket-loads of the stuff. Put the two parsley varieties together, however, and that quite strange, fuzzy texture of the curly parsley just adds something. If you want to make a spur-of-the-moment roast tomato salad to accompany a barbecue, you could char-grill some really sweet tomatoes with some onions and pop these into the salad in place of the slowly roasted tomatoes.

Serves 4–6

10 plum tomatoes, halved
   lengthwise
bunch of mixed herbs (such as sage,
   rosemary, thyme and basil stems)
50 g Maldon salt
2 vine leaves
1 bought or home-made preserved
   lemon (see pages 23–4)
2 handfuls of stoned olives, preferably
   large purple ones
handful of flat-leaf parsley, roughly
   chopped
handful of curly parsley, roughly
   chopped

for the dressing:
3 tablespoons olive oil
2 teaspoons walnut oil
1 tablespoon balsamic vinegar
1 teaspoon lemon juice
½ teaspoon sugar
salt and freshly ground black pepper

1 At least 4 hours ahead, roast the
tomatoes: preheat the oven to
110°C/230°F/gas ¼. If you have a
convection oven, fine; if not, wedge the
door ajar with a wooden spoon, so you
can get the air through.
2 Twist and crumple the bunch of
mixed herbs in your hands to release
their aromatic oils. Sprinkle a baking
tray with half the salt, then scatter half
the herbs on top. Lay the tomatoes on
top of that, cut side up, then scatter with
the rest of the herbs and finish with the
rest of the salt.
3 Put in the oven for about 3 hours,
until the tomatoes are crusty on the
outside but still soft on the inside.
Remove and leave to cool.
4 While the tomatoes are in the oven,
place the vine leaves on a rack over a
roasting tray on another shelf and leave
for about 30 minutes until dried out.
Remove and leave to cool, then cut into
thin strips.
5 Cut the peel from the preserved
lemon. Discard the flesh and cut the
peel into thin strips.
6 In a big bowl, gently combine the
tomatoes with the vine leaf strips,
lemon peel, olives and both types of
parsley.
7 Mix together the dressing ingredients,
season to taste and serve separately.

Veggie Salads

I really like the caramelized sweetness of roast vegetables in salads, especially to serve with barbecued meat, so I'll put some chunks of pumpkin or a whole butternut squash into an oven preheated to about 230–250°C/450–475°F/gas 8–9, together with some rosemary sprigs and some unpeeled medium-sized whole onions, for about half an hour or so, until the onions turn a rich brown and start to pop out of their skins and the pumpkin is soft enough for a knife to glide easily through it but firm enough to let you slice off the skin easily.

I cut off the base of the onions, so that they can be squeezed fully out of their skins, then mix them with the pumpkin chunks and some pine nuts, toasted in a dry pan until they are golden brown. In Italy, instead of pine nuts they might use toasted almonds in a salad like this, or even some crumbled amaretti biscuits. I make a dressing with two parts olive oil to one part sweetish vinegar, like a Cabernet Sauvignon vinegar, if you can get it, or sherry vinegar, or a little balsamic mixed with wine vinegar. Alternatively, you can melt a teaspoon of sugar in a pan with a little water and add that to your usual vinegar. I season the whole thing with plenty of black pepper and mix in a good handful of chopped parsley.

Sometimes, especially when it is one of many dishes, a salad can be as simple as some cauliflower sprigs blanched briefly in boiling water, then drained, allowed to cool and tossed with a mix of sliced red onions and spring onions, some chopped sweet tomatoes, and a few capers. If the capers come in vinegar, you can mix a little of this with olive oil for the dressing; if they are salted, you need to rinse them first, and make up a dressing with olive oil and wine vinegar instead.

When the first tender broad beans come through that can just be shelled and don't need cooking or popping from their outer skins, I like to mix them with sliced green beans that have been blanched briefly in boiling water, then drained and cooled, some chopped spring onions and a handful of chopped flat-leaf parsley. Then I barbecue, grill or pan-fry a piece of smoked haddock or cod until it is crusty on the outside, remove the skin and any bones, break it into shards, and mix it in gently, then dress the whole thing in oil and vinegar.

One of the simplest accompaniments to put out at a barbecue is made from celeriac and carrot chopped into matchstick pieces, mixed in a bowl with some thin slices of spring onion, chopped flat-leaf parsley and some quartered cherry tomatoes, then dressed just with lime juice and seasoned with salt and pepper. Put out a plateful of crispy lettuce leaves, so that people can do as the Vietnamese do and roll up a mound of the really fresh-tasting vegetables inside a lettuce leaf wrapper. One thing to remember with any dressing containing lime juice is that you should use it within an hour or so, otherwise the character of the lime juice changes, and you lose that sharp sourness.

> **I really like the caramelized sweetness of roast vegetables in salads, especially to serve with barbecued meat**

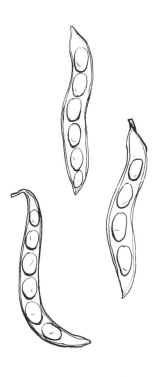

Light

Spicy Crab Salad We get to the really spicy stuff in the next chapter, but I just can't resist including this Thai salad, with a fiery *nam jim* made using ingredients like chillies, garlic and lime juice. This is a really very sexy item on its own, but equally you could serve it with other dishes, especially barbecued whole fish.

I like the dressing to be quite seriously hot, but you can temper it if you prefer by adding less chilli, or by increasing the quantity of palm sugar. The mint leaves in the salad also have a balancing cooling effect. You can make lots of roast coconut at one time and keep what you don't use immediately in an airtight container for later.

Serves 6–8 with other dishes;
4 as a light lunch

25 g fresh coconut flesh
300 g white crab meat
handful of mint leaves, chopped
handful of coriander, chopped
3 lemon grass stalks, stripped of outer
  leaves and thinly sliced
2 large red chillies, deseeded and
  chopped
100 ml Nam Jim (see page 64)

1 Preheat the oven to 190°C/375°F/gas 5.
2 Using a potato peeler, shave the coconut so that it looks like pencil shavings. Scatter them over a baking tray and put them in the oven for about 5 minutes, until they turn golden brown. Keep an eye on them, as they will burn quite quickly.
3 Put the crab meat, herbs, lemon grass and chillies in a bowl with the coconut. Just before serving, add the nam jim dressing and toss everything together.

Seared Scallop, Fennel and Tomato Salad

Buy the biggest scallops in their shells that you can find and ask your fishmonger to shell them for you. The scallops can be pan-fried, or cooked on the barbecue set over some large rosemary twigs.

Serves 4–6

1 fennel bulb, very thinly sliced
about 6 vine tomatoes, quartered
50 g stoned black olives
3 tablespoons lemon juice
3 tablespoons extra-virgin olive oil
good handful of flat-leaf parsley, plus a
  little extra chopped parsley for
  sprinkling
salt and freshly ground black pepper
about 12 large shelled scallops
  (see above)

1 Mix the fennel, tomatoes, olives, lemon juice, oil and parsley. Season to taste.
2 Get a frying pan very hot. Put a little olive oil on a plate, smear your scallops in the oil, then drop them into the hot pan. Leave them alone for about a minute, until they have a lovely golden crust. They should then lift easily from the pan. Flip them over, then, after about 30 seconds, take them out and mix them into the salad.
3 Scatter a little more chopped parsley over the top to serve.

Smoked Bacon Salad with Anchovies and Eggs

If you can find fresh anchovies in vinegar, then use some of this to cut through the richness of the bacon and fried breadcrumbs. If you use anchovies packed in salt, rinse them well before use and add a splash of wine vinegar to the bacon mixture instead. Because of the inherent saltiness of the bacon and anchovies, it is all too easy to overseason this salad, so go very cautiously with any added salt, if you feel the need to add any at all.

Serves 4–6 with other dishes;
2 as a light lunch

200 g smoked lardons or diced streaky
  bacon
1 onion, sliced
2 slices of stale white bread, crumbled
  into small chunks
about 1 tablespoon olive oil
5 anchovies in vinegar or salt,
  roughly chopped
good handful of chopped flat-leaf
  parsley
freshly ground black pepper
dash of wine vinegar (see above)
1 crisp lettuce, washed and separated
  into leaves
4 hard-boiled eggs, shelled and
  quartered

1 Heat a dry frying pan and, when it is hot, put in the lardons. Move them around until they begin to colour, then add the onion slices. When the onion begins to soften and colour, add the bread, with a tablespoon or so of olive oil. Toss everything together and cook until the lardons and bread are golden and quite crisp. Turn off the heat.
2 Mix in the chopped anchovies and parsley. Season with pepper (there should already be enough salt from the bacon and anchovies) and mix in a dash of the anchovy vinegar or a little wine vinegar.
3 Put the lettuce leaves at the bottom of a bowl or plate, set the hard-boiled egg quarters over them, then scatter the bacon mixture on top.

Light

Salad of Mussels, Ginger and Saffron

You can have a great light lunch by preparing a bowlful of ✳ **Moules à la Marinière** cooked in the traditional fashion by sweating some chopped garlic and shallot in butter in a big heavy-based pan, then adding the cleaned and scrubbed mussels and a little white wine, putting on the lid and placing the pan over a fierce heat, shaking all the time until they steam open. Remove the mussels, keep them warm and bubble up the liquid until it thickens (some people add a dash of double cream), then add some chopped parsley. Alternatively you could add chopped fennel, celery and some ginger and saffron, and chill the whole lot...

Serves 4–6

pinch of saffron threads
1.5 kg mussels
a little olive oil
1 fennel bulb, chopped
about 3 celery stalks, chopped
1 onion, chopped
2 shallots, chopped
500 g ripe plum tomatoes
3 garlic cloves, chopped
25 g ginger, chopped
large handful of coriander (with roots),
    chopped, plus extra leaves for garnish
about 1 teaspoon lemon juice
a little extra-virgin olive oil
salt and freshly ground black pepper

1 Put a dry pan on to heat. When it is hot, take it off the heat, put in the saffron and move the threads around for a moment or two until they turn quite dark in colour and release their characteristic aroma.

2 Clean and scrub the mussels in several changes of running water, removing any beards and barnacles and discarding any of the mussels that are open and won't close when they are tapped.

3 Heat the olive oil in a large heavy-based pan. Add the vegetables, garlic and ginger, and cook gently until they soften.

4 Add the mussels and the coriander. Cover the pan with a lid and turn up the heat to high. Keep shaking the pan around until the mussels open. As soon as they do, they are ready. Discard any that refuse to open. Take out the mussels with a slotted spoon and leave to cool.

5 Bubble up the liquid in the pan, adding the roasted saffron. When the liquid has reduced by about half, leave it to cool, then mix with the lemon juice and a little extra-virgin olive oil (the exact amounts will vary according to how much liquor you have left in the pan. It should be about equal parts). Season the dressing to taste with salt and pepper.

6 Pour the dressing over the cool mussels and serve sprinkled with a little extra chopped coriander.

Tarts and Pizzas

On the last day of another holiday in the South of France, I looked at what was left in the fridge and found a slab of puff pastry, some crème fraîche and a bit of bacon. So I made a tart using the pastry spread with crème fraîche, with bacon and shallots scattered on top, baked it until the pastry was golden, then served it with a bowlful of lettuce, some tomatoes, *saucisson* and cheese, and a bottle of chilled wine. What a great way to finish a holiday. You could use puff pastry, or make your own pizza-style base.

French Leave Tart

Makes one 30-cm tart

250 g unbleached white bread flour,
   plus more for dusting
1 teaspoon fresh yeast
1 teaspoon sugar
1 tablespoon olive oil
2 teaspoons salt

for the topping:
275 ml crème fraîche
2 red onions, thinly sliced
250 g smoked lardons or streaky bacon,
   cut into quite thick pieces
freshly ground black pepper

1 Put 50 g of the flour in a bowl with the yeast, sugar, oil and 4 tablespoons water. Mix together and leave for 1 hour, until bubbly and doubled in size.
2 Put in a food processor and, with the machine running, gradually add the remaining flour and salt. Add just enough water to make a soft but not sticky dough (about 2 tablespoons).
3 Preheat the oven to 230°C/450°F/gas 8. Roll the dough out to a round about 30 cm across and place on a baking tray. Spread with crème fraîche, followed by the onions and bacon. Season well with pepper.
4 Bake for 12–15 minutes, until the tart is golden and the base crisp.

You could use the same dough, but roll it out really thinly and make a pizza-style topping of tomato sauce (see page 79). Spread it thinly, then cover with whatever ingredients you like. I often make one with thinly sliced aubergine, prosciutto and mozzarella. Or you could make a ✳**Pissaladière** (the French version of pizza which comes from Nice) with caramelized onions and anchovies. To caramelize the onions, melt 60 g unsalted butter in a large pan, then add 4 large sliced onions, stir until coated with the butter and add 2 tablespoons of red wine vinegar. Cook and continue to stir for about 35–40 minutes, scraping the sides and bottom of the pan, until the onions are caramelized and dry. Spread the onions over the dough base, leaving an edge of around 3 cm, then criss-cross 50 g anchovy fillets over the top, popping a black olive wherever you form a diamond shape, sprinkle with thyme leaves and grind some black pepper over the top. Bake for 20–25 minutes, until the crust is golden brown and risen. Brush with olive oil before you serve it.

Desserts

In France, where you are never far from a *pâtisserie* selling gorgeous glazed open fruit tarts, the idea of making one seems as crazy as making your own baguettes. However, to round off a barbecue or a light lunch back home, it is well worth it. I like to make two or three great big showy tarts, with just one seasonal soft fruit in each, rather than a mixture, but you can be as elaborate as you like. You need to bake a sweet pastry case blind (see page 152), using double the quantity of pastry if you have a big enough tart tin (about 32 cm).

Make up some *crème pâtissière* (see page 97) and mix in an equal quantity of double cream whipped to soft peaks with some sugar (a tablespoon per 200 ml of cream). Spread this over your tart case, then arrange your fruit: raspberries, strawberries, apricots or peaches, or even some fresh figs poached until just soft in a little red wine and sugar then drained and cooled. I like my tarts with the fruit unadorned except for a flurry of icing sugar; if you want to glaze them, however, just melt some apricot or strawberry or damson jam (whichever goes best with your fruit) with a little water in a pan, and brush over the top.

Another thing I could never resist in French *pâtisseries* was ✳ **Pain Perdu**, though it is harder to find these days. Originally it was made with sliced baguette, but done with brioche it is quite beautiful. Just top some thickly sliced brioche with lots of melted butter, followed by slices of apple then soft brown sugar, and put on a baking tray in an oven preheated to 200°C/400°F/gas 6 for about 30 minutes, until it turns golden and you have a wonderful sugary buttery crust.

On a hot day after a barbecue I usually put out bowls of summer fruit: Indian mangoes, really soft and perfumed, sweet over-ripe pineapples, and good peaches that dribble their juice all over your white T-shirt, or tiny wild strawberries, that have so much more flavour than most big strawberries – which can be chalky and grainy and hollow, unless you grow them yourself in the garden. If I'm feeling in the mood I might make some vanilla ice-cream or praline parfait (see overleaf) to serve with them.

> ❛On a hot day after a barbecue I usually put out bowls of summer fruit: Indian mangoes, really soft and perfumed, sweet over-ripe pineapples, and good peaches that dribble their juice all over your white T-shirt❜

Vanilla Ice-cream

Serves 4–6

8 egg yolks
225 g caster sugar
500 ml milk
300 ml double cream
1 vanilla pod

1 In a bowl, whisk the egg yolks with the sugar until pale.
2 Put the milk into a heavy-based pan with half the double cream and the vanilla pod, and bring to just under the boil. Take the pan off the heat.
3 Remove the vanilla pod and then add the milk mixture slowly to the egg and sugar mixture, whisking all the time.
4 Return to the pan and cook over a very low heat until the mixture thickens.
5 Remove the pan from the heat and whisk in the remaining cream. Leave the mixture to cool.
6 When cold, churn in an ice-cream maker, according to manufacturer's instructions, until frozen.

Light

Praline Parfait

The blitzed praline gives a lovely nutty, grainy texture to the parfait. You could also put it out as it is, smashed into largish pieces – but watch your teeth!

You can make rum and raisin parfait in the same way, omitting the praline but stirring in 80 g raisins that have been plumped up for an hour or so in 150 ml rum warmed and sweetened with 1 tablespoon of sugar.

Serves 4–6

80 g caster sugar
4 eggs, plus 1 extra egg yolk
few drops of vanilla extract
400 ml double cream

for the praline:
400 g caster sugar
2 heaped tablespoons hazelnuts
2 heaped tablespoons blanched
  almonds
butter, for greasing

1 Put the caster sugar into a heavy-based pan with a tablespoon of water and let it dissolve into a syrup.

2 Put the eggs and extra yolk into a stainless-steel bowl over a pan of barely simmering water and gradually whisk in the sugar syrup until the mixture is thick and white, then whisk in the vanilla extract. Remove from the heat.
3 Slightly whip the cream until it begins to thicken and fold into the egg mixture.
4 Make the praline: put the sugar into a heavy-based pan and heat very gently until it turns to a golden caramel. Cook to the point where it begins to darken, take off the heat and add the nuts.
5 Grease a shallow tray with butter and line with baking paper. Pour the mixture over the top and spread it out well. Leave it at room temperature for about 1½ hours until it sets.
6 Turn the praline out on a clean work surface and smash it into chunks, then blitz in a food processor until it becomes like fine sand. Keep a handful back and mix the rest into the parfait mixture.
7 Spoon the parfait mixture into a loaf tin or pâté dish and put into the freezer for a few hours until firm.
8 Slice into wedges to serve, sprinkling the rest of the praline on top.

Light

Passion Fruit Pavlova

For me, a barbie isn't a barbie without a big passion fruit pavlova to finish. Maybe you can't really call it light, but outside on a sunny day – after barbecued fish and lamb and salad – is absolutely the best time to eat it. I just love the unctuous sweet meringue, all crispy on the outside and soft like a marshmallow inside, against the sharpness of the passion fruit and the crunch of the seeds. You could make it with berries or mango, but for me this is the best.

Serves 8–10

whites of 12 eggs
2 teaspoons vanilla essence
400 g caster sugar
2 teaspoons white wine vinegar
500 ml double cream
6 tablespoons thick natural yoghurt
10 passion fruit

1 Preheat the oven to 130°C/275°F/gas 1.
2 Make the meringue by whisking the egg whites (preferably by hand, see page 154) with the vanilla essence and half of the caster sugar until it forms soft peaks. Whisk in the rest of the caster sugar, a little at a time, then add the white wine vinegar and a tablespoon of boiling water and continue to whisk until the meringue mixture is stiff and shiny.
3 On a baking sheet, spoon the mixture into a large circular shape, making a big hollow in the centre. Bake for 45–60 minutes, until the meringue is crisp on the outside but still nice and soft inside. Leave to cool.
4 Whisk the double cream and yoghurt together until the mixture is really thick, then spoon it inside the meringue case. Scoop out the seeds and pulp from the passion fruit and pile them on top of the creamy filling.

'A barbie isn't a barbie without a big passion fruit pavlova to finish'

Spicy

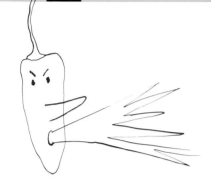

I love spicy food, and there are days when nothing else will do. Spicy food for me means Thai... some Chinese, Malaysian and Singaporean dishes, and a few favourite Indian ideas, but mainly Thai – surely one of the most sensual cuisines in the world. You have to marvel at the intelligence of cooking techniques that can create such a range of flavours from four basic sensations: sweet, sour, salty and hot. Outside Thailand we haven't really got to know many of them yet, dishes like crispy fish salads that are so hot to a Westerner that the first mouthful really hurts, before the balancing effect of the different taste sensations takes over.

What excites people about Thai food is that it is so exhilarating, because the flavours are so pure and clean. When you eat a bunch of fiery fresh chillies, they can have an amazing effect. Your head becomes light and you feel quite euphoric, as if you are being lifted off the ground. There is a wonderful, tingling satisfaction that goes through the whole of your mouth, throat, ears and nose – and, if you are really lucky, it gets to your fingers and toes! The chillies release endorphins, the brain's natural opiates – the more you have the more you want; and the more you eat, the more you can take.

You have only to serve up a big bowl of curry, a spicy salad and a dish of rice and you have a talking point. In Thailand, of course, the balance would be different: there would be a big pot of rice and probably at least seven small dishes – always an odd number – each of which would be tasted separately. Odd numbers are considered lucky in Thai culture. Count the number of steps outside palaces and big hotels and they will invariably be odd, and old recipes will usually have odd numbers of ingredients, such as a finger of galangal or a knuckle of ginger, three lime leaves and three stalks of lemon grass.

> **❝ When you eat a bunch of fiery fresh chillies, they can have an amazing effect. Your head becomes light and you feel quite euphoric, as if you are being lifted off the ground ❞**

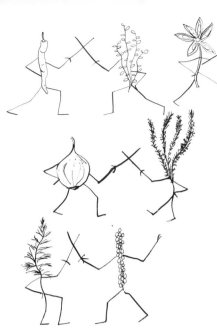

I first came across Asian food in Melbourne, when I worked part-time on Saturdays and Sundays at a restaurant in the suburb of Richmond. Across the road was a big block of flats, where a huge influx of Vietnamese boat people had settled. Suddenly Asian supermarkets started opening up all around. I was twenty years old, and I remember walking into a Vietnamese store and pointing excitedly at things and saying, 'What's that – and what's that?' I tasted sticky rice stuffed with sweet red beans and wrapped in lotus leaves for the first time, and I bought ingredients like lemon grass and daikon radish, took them home and thought, 'What do I do with these?' What a learning curve.

At that time the real explosion of Asian food had yet to happen, and most Australians were still into big steaks and other carnivore dishes, or the Australian version of a Chinese meal – omelette and chips with sweet-and-sour sauce. The only curries I had ever tasted at home were the strange affairs I guess everyone remembers, served with bowls of raisins, sliced banana, chopped pineapple, roasted desiccated coconut and overcooked rice. The restaurants in which I'd trained were French and Italian, and it was about a year before I went to a Japanese restaurant for the first time and discovered mirin and sake and miso, but by then all my thoughts on food were changing completely.

Unfortunately, the next big thing in Australia was the craze for outrageous fusion food. While a sensitive bringing together of, say, Japanese and French ideas can be beautiful, we are talking real mongrel stuff here – a dozen wildly different flavours fighting on a plate, Chinese, Thai, French, Italian, you name it – why we did it I don't know. My feeling is that every ingredient in a classic dish that has been passed down from family to family over thousands of years, contributes something and should be respected. Of course, cooking evolves and changes, and half the fun is in adapting and inventing little twists that stamp your own character on a dish. Sure, if I have a little paste left over from a green curry I might play around with smearing it over some fish, wrap it in coconut leaves and put it on the barbie, because that feels to me like something a Thai person might do. But I wouldn't put chorizo in a Thai curry or make 'Asian pesto' – sweet basil works with pecorino and pine nuts, aniseedy Thai basil just doesn't.

The other joy of cooking Asian food is the shopping for and learning about new ingredients, comparing brands, finding out which you like best. Most towns have an Asian population, with stores catering for the community. If you are stuck, ring up the nearest Thai or Chinese restaurant and ask them where they get their produce. With any luck, they'll put you on to a wholesaler, or they might even say, 'Why don't you buy it from us?'

The reason that people are often mystified by spicy food is that most of us have never really been taught how to taste properly. When I started out as an apprentice, the head chef would say, 'Needs more salt, doesn't it?' and I'd sheepishly say yes, without any idea of what I was supposed to be tasting. Then one day someone said to me, 'This is how the mouth works and you have to understand that before you can move on to the next step.'

❛The next big thing in Australia was the craze for outrageous fusion food... we are talking real mongrel stuff here – a dozen wildly different flavours fighting on a plate❜

All good cooking is about balance, but with Asian food it is particularly rewarding to understand what is going on with your taste buds. Then you can adjust the sweetness, sourness, saltiness or heat, according to your own taste, because everyone's chilli tolerance is different, every chilli has a different level of heat, and everyone's idea of the perfect balance will be slightly different.

If a Thai dish is really working for you, your whole mouth will be completely full of flavour. The first place you will feel the tingling and bubbling sensation is the inside of your cheeks. The tip of your tongue will latch on to the sourness, and you will start to feel the heat at the back and the roof of the mouth, then the lips.

If the balance feels wrong, take a little of your sauce and put it into a bowl. If it is not hot enough, try adding a little more salt, which will bring out the heat of the chillies. If it's too hot, add a little sugar, which will reduce the heat. If it is too sweet, try a little more of your sour ingredient, usually lime juice or tamarind water. If it is not salty enough, add a little fish sauce. Keep a note of what you are adding and, when you are happy with the flavours, use your tasting bowl as a blueprint for the main dish.

Play around with this first recipe for stir-fried squid in a classic Thai *pad prik*, and you will see what I mean about balance. It should be hot, because that is the nature of the dish, but you might like it a little sweeter, or even hotter still.

Pad Prik King with 'Lucky' Squid In the opening sequence of the wonderful Ang Lee film *Eat Drink Man Woman*, the old chef Mr Chu is preparing one of his extraordinary elaborate Sunday lunches. In the middle of all the steaming and hanging of ducks and deep-frying of pork, he scores a sheet of pearly squid on a wooden block, using his cleaver in close lines with devastating speed and accuracy – chok, chok, chok... It's all over in a moment, but it is beautiful to watch.

That scene changed for ever the way I prepare the squid for this dish. I used to make the diagonal cuts quite far apart, but old Mr Chu's technique of fine criss-crossing helps the pieces of squid to curl themselves up quite dramatically, like little fir cones, when they are put into sizzling oil. In Thailand, when the squid curls like that it is supposed to be lucky, hence the name of the dish.

This is an old recipe which quite unusually uses pork fat rather than oil. This tells me that it was probably a royal recipe, as in Buddhist cultures beasts would be sacrificed only for a ceremonial occasion. *Pad* means paste, *prik* means chilli, *king* is ginger – which is odd, because the recipe uses galangal. For me, this is the best squid dish ever; it all works so well – the texture of the squid and the sweetness and heat of the paste, which is not unlike a red curry paste, except that palm sugar and fish sauce are cooked into it from the beginning.

Of course, to have squid in a dish is very decadent for a Thai, so it would be made only in small portions for serving with other dishes like raw vegetables, perhaps a *Tom Kha Kai* – a coconut and chicken soup (seepage 59) – a red or green curry and some crispy fried rice cakes.

Spicy

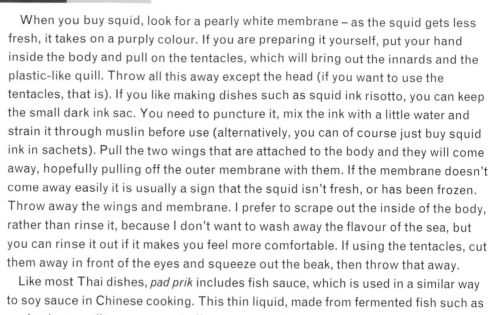

When you buy squid, look for a pearly white membrane – as the squid gets less fresh, it takes on a purply colour. If you are preparing it yourself, put your hand inside the body and pull on the tentacles, which will bring out the innards and the plastic-like quill. Throw all this away except the head (if you want to use the tentacles, that is). If you like making dishes such as squid ink risotto, you can keep the small dark ink sac. You need to puncture it, mix the ink with a little water and strain it through muslin before use (alternatively, you can of course just buy squid ink in sachets). Pull the two wings that are attached to the body and they will come away, hopefully pulling off the outer membrane with them. If the membrane doesn't come away easily it is usually a sign that the squid isn't fresh, or has been frozen. Throw away the wings and membrane. I prefer to scrape out the inside of the body, rather than rinse it, because I don't want to wash away the flavour of the sea, but you can rinse it out if it makes you feel more comfortable. If using the tentacles, cut them away in front of the eyes and squeeze out the beak, then throw that away.

Like most Thai dishes, *pad prik* includes fish sauce, which is used in a similar way to soy sauce in Chinese cooking. This thin liquid, made from fermented fish such as anchovies, smells pungent and off-putting neat, but when mixed with other ingredients it mellows and adds one of the four flavours of Thai cooking, saltiness. Fish sauce is one of the oldest sources of salt. Even the ancient Romans used a type of fish sauce. I think the best Thai fish sauce is Squid brand, which you can buy for the equivalent of a few pence in Thailand, and is exported relatively cheaply in big bottles that will keep for quite a long time, letting the sauce darken and mature gently.

Serves 4 with other dishes

100 g pork fat or around 120 ml
   vegetable oil, plus more for the wok
100 g palm sugar
5 teaspoons fish sauce
300 g medium-sized squid, cleaned
about 5 lime leaves
good handful of Thai basil

for the paste:
9 large red (serrano) chillies
10 g dried red chillies
30 g dried red shrimps
1 medium red onion, chopped
17 garlic cloves
70 g galangal, chopped
10 g coriander roots, chopped
3 lemon grass stalks, stripped of outer
   leaves and chopped

1 First make the paste: slit the fresh chillies down the centre with a sharp knife and use the handle of a small spoon like a shovel to push out all the seeds, then chop the chillies.

2 Snap the stalk end from the dried red chillies and shake out the seeds. Put the dried chillies into a bowl and cover with hot water. Leave for about 30 minutes until they have plumped up.

3 Soak the dried shrimps in cold water, also for 30 minutes.

4 Drain the rehydrated chillies and shrimp, put them in a blender with all the other ingredients and process (or pound them in a mortar with a pestle) until you have a rough paste. You may need to add a little water to bring the paste together, but try to add as little as possible as the ingredients, particularly

the soaked chillies and shrimps, will contain their own moisture.

5 Heat the pork fat or vegetable oil in a heavy-bottomed pan and add the paste. Cook it very slowly, taking care that it doesn't catch on the bottom of the pan, for about 2 hours until all the moisture disappears. Halfway through cooking, add the palm sugar and 1 tablespoon of the fish sauce. When the paste is ready it will be very aromatic and the colour will have deepened to a rich red-brown. Take it off the heat and keep it on one side until you are ready to cook your squid.

6 To prepare the squid, slit the bodies lengthwise and open out into sheets. Place, insides upwards, on a chopping board. Using a very sharp knife or a cleaver at a 45-degree angle, score the squid almost through diagonally one way in a series of cuts about half a centimetre apart, then turn the squid round and repeat at right angles to the first cuts, so you finish up with a diamond pattern. Cut each squid body into decent-sized pieces (about 6 x 4 cm).

7 Now get the wok really hot and add a film of oil. When the oil is really hot, put in the squid pieces, scored side downwards, with the tentacles if you are using them. The secret is to leave the squid pieces for a moment to seal before attempting to move them. They will colour slightly and curl up completely to resemble small fir cones. If the oil isn't hot enough, the squid won't cook quickly enough and liquid may leech out. If this happens, drain off the liquid and put the wok straight back on the heat.

8 Add about 2 tablespoons of your paste to the wok, together with the remaining fish sauce and stir everything around well to coat the squid.

9 Fold the lime leaves in half and pull out the stalk, which is too stringy to eat raw, then chop the leaves quite finely. Chop the basil. Sprinkle both on top of the squid and serve immediately.

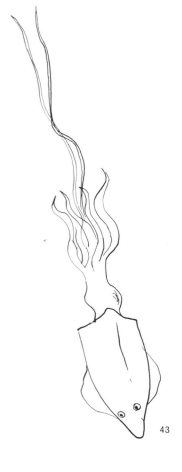

'Old Mr Chu's technique of fine criss-crossing helps the pieces of squid to curl themselves up quite dramatically, like little fir cones, when they are put into sizzling oil'

✳ **Pad Prik King with Crispy Pork** is also a great dish. Steam a piece of pork shoulder for about 30 minutes, then let it get cold and slice it into thin strips. Put a good centimetre of vegetable oil in your wok and deep-fry the pork until the skin is really golden and crispy and the pork properly heated through. Add your *pad prik*, stir it around until it is well heated through, then scatter the dish with chopped lime leaves and Thai basil.

Thai basil is a probably the most distinctive variety of basil and there are around forty types. It is less silky than sweet basil, with a purply tinge and a huge flavour, very strongly aniseedy. I once did an experiment with a dish of spaghetti with red onions and prawns that should be finished with chopped sweet basil. Instead I used Thai basil and the reaction of the people who tasted it was amazing: mostly they thought I had added fennel.

The other basil used exclusively in Thai cooking is Holy basil, which is such a strange herb it is hard to believe it is really part of the basil family at all. Quite furry on the outside, with a prickly texture and a quite pungent flavour, it is used in dishes where it will be cooked for some time, rather than chopped and added at the end. Incidentally, Thai and Holy basil never last in the fridge. The best way to store them is in a cool place wrapped in damp paper, moistened again from time to time.

The Curries
In Asian cooking, the word for 'curry' is synonymous with 'gravy'. In Indian it is *kaari*; in Thai *kaeng*. I reckon that says a lot about the way a curry is designed to be eaten in these countries. In India and Thailand, curries tend to be made with small pieces of meat and lots of 'gravy', and served with about three parts rice to one part curry. In Thailand, curries are prepared quite quickly, while further down the coast in Indonesia curries like *rendang* (see page 54) are cooked long and slow in earthenware pots, rather than woks, until the gravy thickens to a glutinous paste around almost-melting meat.

Before the Europeans brought spoons and forks to Thailand, the way to eat these soupy curries was with balls of sticky rice moulded in your fingers, and this is still the way it is done in many homes. No chopsticks, because the Thais like to distinguish their culture from the Chinese, and a Thai person will never use a knife because a knife on a table is seen as a weapon – a threat.

In countries and regions of the world where people have had to eke out very little meat, you often find the most miraculous combinations of flavours from humble ingredients. Poor families in France, for instance, would make a *pot-au-feu* to last several days and it would have a very small ratio of meat to sauce. If there was only one sausage and a piece of pork, everyone would have a share. The real value of the meat, however, would be in flavouring the pot of vegetables and herbs and sauce that made up the bulk of the meal.

In Thailand, a big pot of curry will be eaten throughout the day as family come and go, helping themselves to handfuls of sticky rice, which will be also on the go all day, inside bamboo steamers. The flavour of the curry comes from the paste that

forms the base of the 'gravy' and which was originally made by pounding whatever herbs, spices and ingredients were to hand, like chillies, kaffir lime leaves and coriander root. If you have only two chicken legs in the fridge, you can still put your heart into making that curry sauce and cooking up a big bowl of rice, and the resulting meal will be memorable.

There are two major Thai curry pastes: red and green. Every Thai family has their own recipe, and the markets sell freshly made ones, all subtly different. The less common yellow curries are milder, made from a curry paste using yellow chillies and often mixed with fish or vegetables and tamarind water to make a 'sour' curry.

The curry pastes are traditionally used in two ways, to make either a jungle curry or a city curry, which is really just another way of saying northern- or southern-style curries. A jungle curry is a northern dish, made with whatever was around in the countryside up towards the Burmese border, usually quite strongly flavoured meats like guinea fowl, wild boar, goat, wild birds – and no coconut milk, because very few coconuts are grown up in the mountains. The city curry is the kind best known in the west: a dish from southern Thailand, lighter, usually made with chicken, pork, beef or fish, and always plenty of coconut milk, because the south is where the big coconut groves are to be found. Of course, these days there are hybrids, what a Thai cookery teacher would call 'suburban curries', that have evolved from people eating out in restaurants and wanting the stronger-flavoured meats associated with jungle curries, but with the sweeter, creamier flavour you get from the coconut milk, rather than the often fierce heat of the jungle curry.

Green curry paste is made with fresh long green chillies; red paste with crushed long dried red chillies; yellow paste with fresh long yellow chillies. Most people make the colour association and assume that red curry is the fieriest; in fact, it is the other way around. Red is always more subtle, and yellow is gentler still. It is the green curry paste that is the serious, blow-your-head-off stuff.

The more chilli you eat, the more heat you can cope with. On one trip I ate jungle curries up near the Burmese border, where they would chop up a whole handful of the tiniest of the Thai chillies, *prik chee nu*, 'rat droppings' or what I call 'scud' chillies, and throw them in at the end of cooking. At first it was like eating a bowl of rice with lots of chilli juice, but by the time I left I had no problem handling the heat. Absolutely the best way to quell fierce chilli heat is to eat lots of sticky rice. Start drinking water or beer and you are finished. Liquid can't wash away the chilli, but rice acts like blotting paper.

If you don't eat spicy food often, take these curries cautiously; if your body isn't used to the heat it could burn your intestine and cause diarrhoea. If wary of the heat or cooking for people who like varying degrees of chilli, the best thing to do is use less curry paste when you make your curry and then do as the Thais do, make a bowl of ✳ **Nam Prik** and serve it as a condiment for people to add extra heat to their food as they please. This chilli sauce has many guises, but at its simplest it can just be chopped small red and green chillies with fish sauce in a bowl. In Thailand it will even be on the breakfast table, for adding to your rice soup.

> ❝Absolutely the best way to quell fierce chilli heat is to eat lots of sticky rice. Start drinking water or beer and you are finished. Liquid can't wash away the chilli, but rice acts like blotting paper❞

When you've been handling chillies, remember to wash your hands – first in just cold water, then using soap. If you use hot water first, you will open up the pores to the alkali in the chillies and end up with painful hands.

Apart from chillies, the other essential ingredient in a red or green curry paste is coriander root. I get very upset if I can find only bunches of coriander which have had the roots chopped off, as it is in the roots that you get the biggest concentration of flavour.

There is also an important point to be made about spices. You should always roast whole spices, and ground spices too, unless they are going to be added to hot oil or boiling liquid, not only to release their flavour but to kill off any harmful bacteria they may harbour. Not many people realize that food poisoning can be caused by adding dried spices straight from the jar into dishes which are being cooked at temperatures too low to kill off the bacteria, or sprinkling them into dishes just before serving, without giving them a chance to cook.

Rinse your whole spices first in cold water and dry them well. This gets rid of any dust, which will otherwise burn in the pan and give the spices a bitter taste. Once roasted, grind them finely using a mortar and pestle or an electric grinder.

The Curry Pastes The quantities given will all make about 6 tablespoons, which will produce about 3 average curries for 4 people. Any paste you don't use immediately can be kept for up to 2 weeks in the fridge, or frozen. Alternatively you can cook it in the creamy part of coconut milk (see page 51) until the spices are aromatic. Cooked, it will keep for several months in the fridge.

When you are blending your paste, if you add the ingredients in the order listed, breaking down the most fibrous first, it should all come together smoothly as the ingredients release their natural moisture, binding them together. If you just chuck all the ingredients in at the same time it will be pretty impossible to pound them using a mortar and pestle. Even if you are using a food processor, the paste will be more chunky and you may need to add a little water to make it hold together. The technique used is actually the same as when making a pesto sauce.

Green Curry Paste

50 g coriander seeds
25 g cumin seeds
1 whole blade of mace
1 teaspoon freshly grated nutmeg
9 garlic cloves, chopped
9 Thai or small shallots, chopped
about 15 coriander roots, chopped, plus
 a handful of coriander leaves

19 long green chillies, deseeded
 and chopped
250 g galangal, chopped
5 lemon grass stalks, outer leaves
 removed and inner stalk chopped
2 teaspoons salt
5 lime leaves, stalks removed and
 leaves chopped
100 g shrimp paste
handful of basil leaves

1 Heat a dry frying pan, put in the spices and roast until they begin to colour and release their aromas. Remove from the heat, then grind to a powder in a spice mill or blender.
2 Put the garlic in a blender or pound in a mortar and pestle, then add the shallots and coriander root, followed by the chillies, galangal, lemon grass and salt. Finally add the lime leaves, shrimp paste and the rest of the ingredients. Process or pound until you have a smooth paste.

Red Curry Paste

This is more layered, complex and refined than the quite raw-edged green curry paste, so the shrimp paste is toasted before being blended in, to give it a richer nutty flavour. If you have any banana leaves, wrap the paste in these instead of foil, as they add their own flavour. Try toasting some extra shrimp paste just to sprinkle over a bowlful of cooked rice – the result is really very tasty.

19 long dried red chillies
1 teaspoon coriander seeds
1 teaspoon cumin seeds
1 small piece of fresh mace
5 white peppercorns
2 tablespoons shrimp paste
7 garlic cloves, sliced
7 Thai or small shallots, sliced
15 coriander roots
100 g galangal, peeled and sliced
3 lemon grass stalks, outer leaves
    removed and inner stalk chopped
pinch of salt
7 lime leaves, cut into thin strips
2 tablespoons kaffir lime zest

1 Snap the stalk end from the dried red chillies and shake out the seeds, then soak the chillies in hot water for 30 minutes until they plump up. Drain.
2 Heat a dry frying pan, put in the spices and peppercorns and roast until they begin to colour and release their aromas. Remove from the heat, then grind to a powder in a spice mill or blender.
3 Wrap the shrimp paste in foil and roast in a dry pan until fragrant.
4 Put the garlic and shallots in a blender or mortar, add the coriander roots, chillies, galangal, lemon grass and salt, and process or pound until a paste begins to form. Then add the toasted shrimp paste, the spices and the rest of the ingredients. Blend or pound to a smooth paste.

Yellow Curry Paste

30 g dried shrimps
10 g shrimp paste
3 garlic cloves, chopped
7 red shallots, chopped
50 g galangal, chopped
19 long yellow chillies, deseeded and
    chopped
2 teaspoons salt
20 g fresh turmeric

1 Soak the dried shrimps in water for about 30 minutes.
2 Wrap the shrimp paste in foil and roast in a dry pan until fragrant.
3 Put the garlic and shallots in a blender or pound in a mortar, then add the galangal, chillies and salt, followed by the shrimp paste, drained shrimps and turmeric. Blend to a paste.

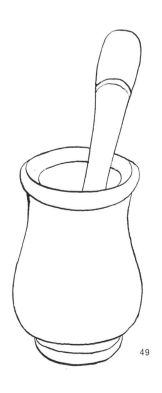

Vegetable Jungle Curry

The use of Shaoxing wine in this recipe shows the Chinese influence creeping in. The long snake beans are similar to stringless green beans but crunchier; substitute green beans if you can't find them. Krachai stalks, looking like a bunch of fingers, are a cross between ginger and galangal, but a bit sweeter and with a peppery bite. Krachai is available in Asian supermarkets, but you can use ginger if you can't get it.

Serves 6–8

150 ml vegetable oil
1–2 tablespoon(s) Green Curry Paste (see page 48)
5 tablespoons fish sauce, plus more to taste
2 litres chicken stock
100 ml Shaoxing wine
200 g snake beans or green beans, cut into pieces
11 small green aubergines, halved
200 g bamboo shoots, cut into pieces
bunch of Thai basil
100 g Krachai stalks or root ginger, peeled and cut into strips
29 kaffir lime leaves, torn

1 Heat the oil in a wok or large pan. Stir-fry the curry paste for a few minutes until fragrant. Add the fish sauce and continue to fry for another minute.
2 Add the remaining ingredients, simmer for a few minutes to soften the beans, then turn off the heat and leave to rest for 5 minutes to allow the flavours to infuse before serving.

Yellow Jungle Curry of Fish and Bamboo Shoots

Serves 4–6

1–2 tablespoon(s) Yellow Curry Paste (see page 49)
handful of sliced bamboo shoots
200 g snake or green beans, cut into pieces
1 small fresh pineapple, peeled, cored and cut into chunks
2 tablespoons fish sauce
2 tablespoons tamarind water (tamarind pulp soaked in water and squeezed)
1 tablespoon palm sugar
500 g skinless fillets of meaty white fish, such as cod, monkfish, John Dory, cut into chunks
500 ml fish stock or water
1–2 tablespoon(s) lime juice
handful of Thai basil, to garnish

1 Bring a little water to the boil in a wok or large saucepan. Add the yellow curry paste and cook for a few minutes until the flavours of the paste's constituents are released.
2 Add the bamboo shoots and beans, and stir around for about 5 minutes until well coated.
3 Add the pineapple, fish sauce, tamarind water and sugar. Cook for about 3 minutes.
4 Add the fish and stock or water and continue to bubble until cooked through, about 3–5 minutes.
5 Remove from the heat and stir in the lime juice. Add some more fish sauce to taste, if necessary. Garnish with Thai basil to serve.

The City Curry

In the Bangkok markets you can watch fresh coconut milk being made from the whole nuts. They are stripped of their husks and the flesh is put through a shredding machine. Then it is mixed with water and put into a special muslin sack which goes into a hydraulic press. The milk from this first pressing is really creamy. Some of the residue is put through again for a second pressing and this gives a much thinner milk.

Even if you had the patience and brute force to grate and press your own coconut milk in your kitchen at home you would need about 5 coconuts to produce the litre of milk needed for some of the recipes. It's therefore much easier to buy a good-quality Thai brand of coconut milk (sometimes called extract), which is a blend of the two pressings. Don't buy a Singaporean brand, as the milk will usually be thinner, as in Singapore it is used more in soups and noodle dishes and as a drink, rather than in rich curries.

Avoid sweetened coconut milk, which is intended for desserts, and block coconut, which is made from coconut meat and will turn the curry thick and fibrous (it is used for preparations like *lom*, a sweet paste).

When you are making curries, ignore the instructions on the coconut-milk can and don't shake it before you use it. You will then find that the milk has separated and a thick layer of fatty cream will be sitting at the top and clinging to the lid (the other way round if the can has been stored upside down). If you bought a bag of fresh coconut milk in a Thai market you would see the same thing: gradually the milk would split and the fatty cream would stick to the top of the bag.

It is this fatty part which will be used at the start of the curry to fry the curry paste. The rest will be added later. In the restaurant business, oil is sometimes used for frying the paste, because of the large quantities being prepared, but the authentic way doesn't use oil at all.

Cook the paste over a moderate heat – nothing too high or it will burn. The sour raw-shallot, raw-garlic aroma being given off by the mixture will suddenly change into something quite fragrant in which all the ingredients come together. At that point you add the rest of your milk and the other ingredients. After a while, as the curry bubbles, a film of oil will ooze through to the surface of the curry and, provided your meat is cooked through, it is ready.

❝ Even if you had the patience and brute force to grate and press your own coconut milk in your kitchen at home you would need about 5 coconuts to produce the litre of milk needed for some of the recipes ❞

Spicy

City Chicken Green Curry

Don't let green curries carry on cooking once the chicken is ready, otherwise the fresh vibrant green colour will begin to turn grey.

Serves 4–6

two (400-g) cans of coconut milk
2 tablespoons Green Curry Paste
   (see page 48)
800 g skinless chicken thigh fillets, cut
   into 3
7 lime leaves, veins removed and
   shredded
3 lemon grass stalks, outer leaves
   removed and inner stalk chopped
20 g galangal, sliced
1 tablespoon palm sugar
1 tablespoon fish sauce
handful of pea aubergines
bunch of Thai basil

1 Scrape the fatty part of the coconut milk into a warm, but not smoking-hot, wok and cook it slowly, stirring all the time, until it starts to bubble and sizzle and just begins to split.
2 Add the green curry paste and cook for a few moments until it releases its aromas.
3 Add the chicken, the rest of the coconut milk, the lime leaves, lemon grass, galangal, palm sugar and half the fish sauce. Let the sauce bubble for about 15 minutes, until the oil in the coconut milk starts to come through to the surface.
4 Add the pea aubergines and the rest of the fish sauce and cook for a few minutes more.
5 Scatter the Thai basil over the curry and serve.

City Red Pork Curry

In a red curry, the paste can be cooked out a little longer with the palm sugar before adding the meat. The sugar increases the temperature at which the mixture cooks and this helps to draw the flavour out a bit more, without destroying the colour.

Serves 4–6

two (400-g) cans of coconut milk
2 tablespoons Red Curry Paste
   (see page 49)
1 tablespoon palm sugar
800 g boneless pork shoulder, cubed
small handful of lime leaves
1 tablespoon fish sauce
handful of Thai basil
handful of coriander leaves

1 Scrape the fatty part of the coconut milk into a warm, but not smoking-hot, wok and cook it gently, stirring all the time, until it starts to bubble and sizzle and just begins to split.
2 Add the red curry paste and palm sugar and cook for a few moments until they release their aromas.
3 Add the pork and cook for about 5 minutes, then add the rest of the coconut milk and the lime leaves. Let the sauce bubble for about 15 minutes, until the oil in the coconut milk starts to come through to the surface.
4 Add the fish sauce and cook for a few more minutes.
5 Scatter on the Thai basil and coriander to serve.

The sweetness of red curries also works well in a much more delicate dish like ✳ **Prawn and Pumpkin Curry**. For 4 people you would need to clean and prepare about 20 large prawns. Shell them, removing the heads, but leaving their tails intact, then run a knife along the back of each prawn to remove the dark intestinal vein. Peel and chop about 250 g pumpkin. You will need two 400-g cans of coconut milk because this is going to be quite a creamy sauce.

Separate the fatty part of the coconut milk from one can and put this into a wok, stirring until it begins to split, then add just 1 tablespoon of Red Curry Paste (see page 49), as you don't want to overpower the prawns. Stir over a moderate heat for about 5 minutes, until the paste releases its fragrance and is sizzling nicely in the cream.

Then add the coconut cream from the second can with 1 tablespoon of palm sugar and simmer for a few minutes. Add ½ tablespoon of fish sauce (go easy, as the prawns have their own saltiness and you can add more later). Put in the chopped pumpkin, cook for a minute, then add the rest of the coconut milk and simmer until the pumpkin is soft and the oil from the coconut milk starts to come through to the surface.

Drop in the prawns and cook as briefly as you need to, so that they are properly cooked, but not overdone. Scatter on some chopped chillies to taste and a handful of shredded lime leaves.

While most Thai curries are made with small pieces of meat, there is one great exception: ✳ **Red Curry with Roast Duck**. The duck is roasted whole in the classic way (see page 116) and served with the red curry sauce on the side (made in the same way as for the City Red Pork Curry opposite, but with some pea aubergines chucked in at the end) and a big bowl of rice.

Fluffy Rice I love rice, though as a kid I hated it because it always seemed to be overcooked and pulpy. Then a Chinese cook I worked with taught me to make it the way Chinese restaurants do it, with half American long-grain rice and half Thai fragrant rice mixed together to give you the best fluffy rice.

Don't worry about weighing anything: put as many handfuls as you like into a big pot, run water over the rice, stir it around, let it sit for a few moments and then drain it off. Do that three times, then cover the rice with fresh water to come up to the first knuckle on your index finger above the surface of the rice. Add salt, put on the lid, bring it to the boil and boil for 1 minute. Turn the heat off and leave the pot on the hob with the lid on. After 25 minutes you will have perfect rice, which you just fluff up with a fork. It works every time. This is the sort of rice used in restaurants and smarter or more Westernized homes in Thailand, Malaysia and Singapore.

In the north of Thailand in particular, they prefer sticky rice, because it can be eaten more easily with the fingers. The further north you go, the stickier the rice tends to get. In the mountains they grow land rice, well away from the paddy fields, which has a shorter grain and is very sticky.

❛The further north you go, the stickier the rice tends to get❜

Sticky rice should be rinsed twice – not too much or it will lose its stickiness. Put a cloth into a steamer, add your rice, put on the lid and steam for about 3 hours, until soft and sticky. Gather up the cloth and leave it until required. Whether you serve fluffy or sticky rice is really up to you. I love the slight sweetness of sticky rice with salads; but with curries I like quite free rice, as it can then get all mixed up in the sauce.

Beef Rendang with Lemon Grass and Ginger

This Muslim dish from Sumatra cooks down to a kind of beef in jam; the melting meat reminds me of the best meat pies.

Serves 4–6

2 lemon grass stalks
2 tablespoons ground coriander seeds
1 teaspoon cumin seeds
2 tablespoons ground turmeric
100 ml vegetable oil
1 kg onions (about 5 large), finely chopped
8 garlic cloves, chopped
20 g red chillies, deseeded and chopped
100 g ginger, chopped
2 bay leaves
1.5 kg stewing steak, cut into cubes
1 (400-g) can of coconut milk
500 ml strong veal or beef stock

1 Pound the lemon grass in a mortar with a pestle until it is a pulp. Grind the whole spices to a powder.
2 Heat the oil in a large heavy-based pan. Add the onions, garlic, chillies, ginger and lemon grass and cook gently until the onions are softened.
3 Add the spices and bay leaves. Fry for a few minutes more until the mixture is very fragrant.
4 Add the meat and increase heat to brown it well, stirring to coat in the spices.
5 Add the coconut milk and stock, bring to a simmer, cover and leave over a low heat for about 2 hours, until the meat is tender.
6 Turn the heat up to high and continue to cook until the sauce reduces down to a fairly thick paste coating the meat (about 15–20 minutes).
7 Serve with rice.

In Singapore they also make a quite dry curry, with ground spices as well as paste, then stock and/or coconut milk are added and the whole thing reduced down until muddy. They use meat on the bone, unlike the Thais, Malaysians and Indonesians. I make my ✳**Singapore Dry Curry** by pounding a good-sized piece of ginger into a paste with around 10 deseeded dried red chillies, rehydrated for about 30 minutes in hot water then drained, a couple of garlic cloves and about 8 Thai shallots. I fry the paste in about 2 tablespoons of oil for about 3–5 minutes, until fragrant, then add 2 teaspoons ground coriander, 1 teaspoon each of ground cumin and ground turmeric and a pinch of fenugreek, and fry for another 2 minutes or so. Next I add about a kilo of chicken pieces, such as thighs, and fry for 5 minutes until well coated. Finally I add a shaken can of coconut milk, and a chopped lemon grass stalk. The sauce is then simmered until reduced right down, about 1 hour. Just before serving, I add a squeeze of lime juice and season with salt.

Noodles Everyone I know loves noodles. A big bowl on the table, with some pak choi mixed through them – maybe some tomato sauce and a sausage on the side for Marcel – and my kids are in heaven. I even love pot noodles, at least the serious, spicy kind you buy for breakfast in Japan or Thailand. It is always good fun to explore Asian supermarkets and see what new types of noodle you can find. On one trip to Chinatown I discovered some wonderful soft shards of freshly made noodles, like squid, sold with chopped chillies and spring onions.

The great Thai classic noodle dish is ✳ **Pad Thai**, which you make with a base of equal quantities of garlic, ginger and coriander root, pounded into a paste in a mortar or food processor, then fried in a little oil. You add a handful of chopped fresh prawns, and stir-fry until these are almost cooked through, then drop in some rehydrated rice noodles and fry until the noodles are just soft. Add a little water, drop in 2 eggs, some dried shrimps, chopped spring onions and beansprouts, sprinkle in a little oyster sauce, then toss the whole lot together until the eggs are cooked. Turn out into a bowl and sprinkle with a little dry-roasted dried chilli powder and some chopped coriander leaves. You can also add to the garnish some crushed roasted peanuts and pickled turnip, which can be bought in jars from Oriental stores.

I always have one curry paste or another on the go in the fridge, so whenever we want a quick but really tasty, sticky, spicy dish for a bunch of friends I'll fry some sliced skinless chicken thigh fillets in quite a lot of oil, add the paste, fry it for a few minutes more, add some coconut milk, then toss in some thick cooked noodles.

A really simple Malaysian noodle dish my wife makes for Marcel and Casper all the time is based on a paste of garlic, ginger and coriander root made in the same way as that for Pad Thai and fried in a little vegetable oil. To that is added some cooked Chinese oi noodles, which are stirred around to coat them in the sauce, and then some chopped spring onions and beansprouts are also added. These are fried for another 30 seconds or so, then some thick sweet soy sauce and a little light soy sauce is stirred in. After a bit more stirring around, the contents of the pan are tipped into a bowl and some deep-fried shallots, garlic and chilli, cooked in that order, and some chopped fresh coriander sprinkled on top. It is wonderfully tasty.

The other world-famous noodle dish is the elaborate and gorgeous *laksa*...

Laksa Laksa is a classic Singaporean dish, a quite fancy version of a spicy coconutty dish native to southern Malaysia. It is like a soupy version of coronation chicken sauce, but much more delicious – with soft thick rice noodles mixed through it. Like a Thai curry, the base of the dish is a paste – in fact, an amalgamation of two different pastes – the main difference is that *laksa* is thickened with nuts. Indonesian cooking tends to use peanuts; Malay cooking uses candlenuts, which are quite waxy and rounded and pointy at one end. (You can substitute blanched almonds if you can't find them.) Don't be put off by the seemingly endless list of ingredients that goes into the pastes – they are really simple to make.

Laksa is the kind of dish that has people competing over whose mum makes the best. Often thin and thick noodles are mixed together, but the real opportunity for flamboyance is in the garnish, which can involve anything from the biggest prawns you can find to strips of omelette. Often clams are used instead of prawns, giving an extra salty dimension, or the seafood can be replaced with slivers of cooked chicken. Inevitably the garnish includes beansprouts, the watery volume of which knocks back some of the spice.

Beansprouts are a much maligned ingredient. Personally I love them. In Thailand I bought them fresh in the market from a woman who grew them in a 44-gallon drum with a wet potato sack over the top. People came along and picked their own, feeling around inside the drum to make sure they got the ones they wanted. Those beansprouts were so, so good, with a wonderful nutty flavour I remembered from the days in Australia, when everyone used to grow their own on windowsills from kits.

Because of its layers of texture – soft noodles, creamy sauce, crunchy beansprouts and vegetables – laksa makes a great vegetarian dish if you substitute vegetable stock and leave out the prawns and fish balls. You could instead add some thin strips of red pepper with the rest of the vegetables.

Malay and Singaporean dishes are usually served with a bowl of *sambal* – a paste made with ingredients like fish, chillies, sugar, salt, lime juice (sometimes), tamarind or mango. It is used as a condiment and comes in two types – hot and blow-your-head-off hot. There are many variations. This recipe uses *sambal oeleck*, which can be bought in jars and is made from chillies, sugar and salt.

Seafood Laksa

Serves 4-6

250 g thick (preferably udon) noodles, fresh or dried
one (400-g) can of coconut milk
1¼ litres chicken stock
1 teaspoon fish sauce
sambal oeleck (see above), to serve

for the Laksa Paste:
½ teaspoon coriander seeds
pinch of cumin seeds
1 onion, chopped
50 g root ginger, peeled and chopped
1 lemon grass stalk, outer leaves removed and inner stalk chopped
4 lime leaves, stalks removed and leaves chopped

5 coriander roots, washed and dried
50 g candlenuts or blanched almonds
1 teaspoon shrimp paste
4 garlic cloves
120 ml vegetable oil
1 teaspoon ground turmeric
1 teaspoon ground coriander
2 teaspoons ground cumin
2 large red (serrano) chillies, deseeded and chopped

for the Red Paste:
50 g galangal, chopped
50 g root ginger, peeled and chopped
2 garlic cloves
40 g shrimp paste
100 g Thai shallots, peeled
1 lemon grass stalk, outer leaves removed and inner stalk chopped

4 coriander roots, washed and dried

5 large red (serrano) chillies, deseeded
   and chopped

3 tablespoons vegetable oil

*for the garnish (these are just
   suggestions, use some or all
   as you please):*

25 g tofu, cubed

25 g fish balls (ready-made from an
   Asian store)

vegetable oil, for frying

25 g really big prawns

50 g choi sum, cut into thin strips

50 g Chinese cabbage, cut into thin
   strips

50 g beansprouts

25 g cucumber, cut into thin strips

bunch of coriander leaves, chopped

a little chilli powder

1 Get the noodles ready: if they are
fresh, rinse them in cold water, then dip
them briefly in a big pan of boiling
salted water for just long enough to
heat them through. Drain them and
keep warm. If using dried wheat- or
egg-based noodles, boil them until
soft, drain and keep warm. If using
dried rice noodles, simply rehydrate
them in cold water for 10 minutes,
drain and keep warm.

2 If you are using tofu and fish balls as
a garnish, fry them in a little vegetable
oil on all sides and set aside.

3 If you are using prawns as a garnish,
shell them and run a knife along the
back to remove the dark intestinal vein.
Set aside.

4 To make the Laksa Paste: roast the
coriander and cumin seeds in a dry pan
until they release their aromas and
colour slightly. Grind them to a powder,

then put in a food processor with the
onion, ginger, lemon grass, lime leaves,
coriander root, nuts, shrimp paste,
garlic and 20 ml of the vegetable oil.
Process to a purée.

5 Heat the rest of the oil in a large pan
and add the turmeric, ground coriander
and cumin, and the chillies. Fry for
about 5 minutes, stirring all the time,
until fragrant.

6 Add the spicy onion purée to the pan
and cook, stirring continuously, for 5–8
minutes, until you have a very aromatic
jam-like paste. Set aside.

7 While the purée is cooking, make the
Red Paste: purée all the ingredients
except the oil and then heat the oil in a
wok and fry the purée in it for about 10
minutes until the paste darkens. Add
the Laksa Paste and bubble up until
darkened and quite aromatic.

8 Add the coconut milk, chicken stock
and fish sauce, and bring to the boil.
Then add the prawns and fish balls, if
you are using them, and cook for 5
minutes more.

9 Pour the hot sauce into a big bowl,
then put in the noodles. Garnish with
the tofu, choi sum, Chinese cabbage,
beansprouts and cucumber. Sprinkle
with chopped coriander and a little dry-
roasted chilli powder.

10 Serve the *sambal oeleck* in a small
bowl for people to help themselves.
If they are your good friends, warn
them if you've chosen a blow-your-
head-off type!

❝ **The real
opportunity for
flamboyance is
in the garnish,
which can
involve
anything from
the biggest
prawns you
can find to
strips of
omelette** ❞

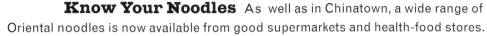

Know Your Noodles

Know Your Noodles As well as in Chinatown, a wide range of Oriental noodles is now available from good supermarkets and health-food stores.

Ming, or wonton, noodles are used by the Chinese, especially in duck noodle soup. Made from wheat, they are yellow and very thin – like hair – and often covered in flour. They cook very quickly, like fresh pasta. Use a ratio of 1 litre of boiling water for every 100 g of noodles and they will float up to the top of the pan when they are done. Don't drain them in a colander, as they will stick together, just pick them up with chopsticks or a pair of forks, drop them into a bowl, then pour soup or sauce over the top. Don't use them for stir-frying as they will then just turn gluey.

Kwei tiao are thick, flat rice noodles used in Chinese, Vietnamese, Singaporean, Malaysian and Thai cooking. The best *rice noodles* are really ricey-flavoured. In Thailand, where they are used particularly for the famous Pad Thai (see page 55), you can buy the noodles laid out fresh in the market. Dried noodles are first soaked in water until rehydrated and softened, then fried in a wok.

Mung bean thread, or glass, noodles are usually used in Chinese soups. They are first soaked in cold water to reconstitute them, then put into a bowl and covered with soup, etc.

Rice vermicelli are used by Thais in *laarps* (traditional offal salads) and other salads, and by the Vietnamese in their spring rolls. These noodles are also soaked in cold water and are rarely cooked, as they will disintegrate, though they can be deep-fried for crispy rice noodle salad. Despite instructions on some packets, never use for stir-frying, as the noodles will just stick together.

Udon are the thick fresh wheat noodles used for *Laksa*. They can be stir-fried or added to sauces. They are also used to make a dessert of sweet noodles: cook them, pour boiling coconut milk over the top to make a sloppy soup or leave it to set and cut it into pieces. It is really tasty!

Oi (or 'oil' in Chinese) is a fresh noodle, coloured white or yellow, made from wheat flour and water, and oily on the outside, used by the Malaysians and Chinese. The white version is thicker, with more of a wormy texture. Oi noodles are used for dishes like noodles with egg and spring onion and oyster sauce. They are also available dried, but are more flavourful fresh.

Soba are Japanese buckwheat noodles that are cooked four times (drained and refreshed in cold water each time) to strengthen them, otherwise they would fall apart, as buckwheat pasta can. They are eaten cold, mixed with mirin, soy and dashi stock, shredded spring onions, and perhaps served with something like tuna.

Soups

Asian cooking is full of fantastic, clean-tasting, clear soups that are all about a quick infusion of powerful, aromatic ingredients, to which you can then add noodles, spring onions and chillies – or even some dumplings and prawns.

One of the classic clear Thai soups is ✳**Tom Yam**, which in its simplest form starts with a pot of boiling water, to which you add hot and sour flavours, beginning with galangal and lemon grass, both chopped roughly and crushed, and a handful of lime leaves that have been torn and crunched in your hands. The heat is then turned down to a simmer and some chopped chillies, tamarind water, fish sauce and palm sugar added.

The pan is taken off the heat, the soup tasted and the flavours adjusted according to whether you want it to be more sweet, sour or hot (remember the balancing act of hot, sour, sweet and salty). Just before serving, some fresh lime juice is added for an extra kick of sourness. It is important that the soup is not allowed to cook any longer or the flavours will change and you will get a cooked citrus taste, rather than the zing of lime juice.

If you want to make a more intensely flavoured soup, use chicken stock instead of water, and elaborate on it with strips of raw fish or prawns, or thin strips of chicken, thrown in for a few minutes at the end to cook through. When chicken is added the soup is called ✳**Tom Yam Kai**, which in turn becomes ✳**Tom Kha Kai** if you make your soup with two parts stock to one part coconut milk.

Duck soup with noodles is one of my favourites. Whenever I roast a duck (see page 116), I then boil up the carcass to make stock, and infuse that with ingredients like sesame oil, ginger and star anise, and add some of the duck meat and some cooked noodles.

If you want a dish that makes a meal for two people, serve this soup in great big bowls, giving each person a sliced duck breast and a leg. Alternatively, strip the meat from the bones (adding the bones to your pot of stock) and chop or shred to make a more delicate soup for more people.

Duck Soup with Noodles
Serves 4-6

1 duck, roasted as described on page 116
5-cm piece of root ginger, peeled
   and sliced
6 star anise
½ teaspoon white peppercorns
large bunch of coriander, with roots
2 tablespoons dark sesame oil
3 tablespoons fish sauce
8 spring onions, thinly sliced

about 50–150 g (25–75 g raw weight per person) cooked ming noodles
sliced chillies to taste, optional

1 Remove the legs and breasts from the duck, and cut into portions, slicing or shredding as you please (see above).
2 Chop the duck carcass into 4 or 5 pieces and put in a large pan. Cover with about 4 litres of water and bring to the boil. Skim off any fat and impurities from the surface.

3 Turn the heat down to a simmer and add the ginger, star anise and peppercorns. Leave to simmer gently for 1–2 hours, skimming the surface regularly to remove any fat and impurities, until the stock has reduced by about half.

4 Meanwhile, pick the leaves from the coriander and reserve. Wash, dry and chop the stem and roots, and reserve separately.

5 When the stock has reduced sufficiently, strain it through a fine sieve into a clean pan. Bring back to the boil, then reduce the heat to a gentle simmer.

6 If you are adding large pieces of duck, put them in for long enough to make sure they are properly heated through; if you are adding smaller chopped or shredded pieces, add them in at the end as they will need very little time.

7 Add the sesame oil and the fish sauce. Crush the coriander roots lightly and add to the pot. Turn off the heat and leave to infuse for a further 5 minutes or so before serving.

8 Just before serving, add the sliced spring onions, noodles and chillies, if you are using them.

9 Ladle out the duck and divide, with the noodles, between warmed bowls, then pour the soup over the top. Scatter the tops of the bowlfuls with some coriander leaves.

❝ I learned to chop crispy-skinned duck and pork by looking through Chinatown restaurant windows, watching chefs wield their cleavers on wooden blocks ❞

Green Papaya Salad

In most areas of Thailand you'll find street stalls selling *som tum*, the classic salad made with crushed green papaya, dried shrimps, lots of chillies, palm sugar, lime juice and coriander. Young kids sit on the streets peeling the green papayas, which hang everywhere in the trees like jewels. They peel them with a little knife, as if they were carving wood. Then, with a big knife, they chop the papayas really fast, first one way then the other, then hold the fruit upright and slice it very thinly, so the flesh tumbles into a mound of cubes. Finally they pound the papaya in a big mortar with a pestle.

Everyone in Thailand knows just how they like their *som tum*, so the stallholder – sometimes the same young boy or girl – will stand there saying, 'More chilli, more sugar, more lime juice?' That is, of course, once you have convinced them that you are really serious about flavour. Often when they spot a tourist they'll say, '*Ferang, ferang*', which literally means 'no flavour' – it is also the colloquial term for 'white man'!

On one visit to Chiang Mai in northern Thailand I tasted a *som tum* that almost blew me away. With every breath I took it felt hotter and hotter, until my eyes and nose started to stream. I'd never experienced anything like it. Fortunately the *som tum* stall is never far from the sticky rice stall, where you can buy your rice in little pieces of cellophane, roll it up into small balls in your fingers and use it to blot out some of the heat in the salad.

For this particular papaya salad that follows I have moved the *som tum* idea on a bit by combining it with another Thai recipe for duck braised in coconut milk. The recipe is originally for beef, and works brilliantly with all those quite sinewy trimmings with which you can't otherwise do very much. When you cook meat in this way, the coconut milk breaks it down and changes it into something gelatinous and delicious.

You could use the cooking method for any meat you like, except lamb, which doesn't work at all in Asian-style food. As far as the Thai people are concerned, lamb stinks – and when you pit its quite sweet, rich flavour against the sharp, fresh flavours of lemon grass, lime leaves, basil and chilli, you can appreciate their point. I did try a lamb salad once; it was disgusting because, when it cools down, the fat sets and coats the top of your mouth when you eat it.

Before the duck is braised, it is first 'washed' in some fish sauce and then it is left overnight. This is the same technique that is used for strips of pork, which are later fried and sliced into stir-fries, with vegetables like *gai lan*, a Chinese flowering broccoli.

After a few hours of braising, the fat in the coconut milk works on the texture of the duck to produce meat as melting and flavoursome as the best moist *confit*, so that it breaks away from the bone in big chunks, like roast chicken. The skin, which by now is packed with flavours, is dried out a little bit more over a rack in the oven until it is really crisp, then crumbled up and sprinkled over the top of the salad, as a tasty condiment.

61

Spicy

Spiced Duck Salad

You need only a little roast rice in this recipe to add an extra crunch along with the beans, but it is worth roasting a jar full and keeping them to pop into any salad.

I prefer to cut the papaya into strips, rather than pound it, as is more traditional in Thailand.

Serves 8

4 duck legs
3 tablespoons fish sauce
about 50 g Thai fragrant rice
about 10-cm piece of galangal
3 lemon grass stalks
11 lime leaves
100 ml coconut milk

3 green papayas or Thai green mangoes), peeled and cut into julienne strips
25 g raw snake beans or string beans, finely chopped
25 g Chinese cabbage, thinly sliced
5 long red (serrano) chillies, deseeded and finely chopped
bunch of Thai basil

for the dressing:
1 red and 1 green Thai chilli
2 tablespoons fish sauce
2 tablespoons lime juice
2 tablespoons palm sugar
1 tablespoon tamarind water (see page 50)

The day before:

1 Rub the duck all over with the fish sauce and leave it, skin side down, in this marinade for about 12 hours or preferably overnight.

Next day:

2 Preheat the oven to 220°C/425°F/gas 7.

3 Put the rice into a bowl and cover with water. Leave for about 5 minutes, then drain. Scatter it evenly over a baking sheet and roast for about 30 minutes, until the grains turn off-white and begin to pop and become 'nutty' in flavour. Crush lightly in a mortar with a pestle

4 Shake excess marinade from the duck and put in an ovenproof dish with the galangal, lemon grass and 3 lime leaves. Pour the coconut milk over the top.

5 Put into the oven and cook for about 2 hours, then turn the oven down to 180°C/350°F/gas 4 and cook for another hour, until the duck meat is cooked and falls away from the bone easily.

6 Remove the skin and place it on a rack over a roasting pan. Put it in the oven for about 30 minutes, until the skin is dry and crisp. Crumble and reserve.

7 In a large bowl, combine the papaya, beans, cabbage, chillies, the remaining lime leaves cut into strips, the basil and the roasted rice.

8 Shred the duck meat and add to the salad.

9 At the last minute, combine all the dressing ingredients, pour over the salad and toss to coat.

Spicy

Lamb might not be acceptable in a Thai salad, but ✳**Kangaroo Salad** is delicious, the meat seared in a hot wok and left to cool, then sliced thinly and mixed with chopped lime leaves, chopped long red chillies, coriander, Thai basil and beansprouts. You can also pepper the kangaroo, rolling it in crushed white peppercorns (with the choking dust sieved off first) before searing it. If you don't have any kangaroo to hand, beef will do just as well!

The salad is dressed with ✳**Nam Jim**, a classic dressing which is a real beauty, as simple an example of hot, sour, salty and sweet as you can find. As always, you can experiment with it and make it as hot as you like. My basic recipe is for 2 garlic cloves, 3 coriander roots and 3 'scud' chillies, all pounded in a mortar with 1 tablespoon of fish sauce and 3 tablespoons each palm sugar and freshly squeezed lime juice (about 3 limes). Remember always to use fresh lime juice as soon as possible and definitely within 2 hours, as after that it will change its character and lose its sharpness.

Salt and Pepper Prawns with Roast Chilli Dressing

White or green peppercorns were used to produce heat in Asian food before the Portuguese introduced chillies, and salt and pepper prawns is a Singaporean idea, which also uses garlic in the most delicious way. The whole bulb is crushed, skin on, with white peppercorns using a mortar and pestle. This is then fried until it goes gorgeously sticky, and then mixed with the prawns, coriander and a chilli dressing that is actually classically Thai but I think in this case is an acceptable fusion. The distinctive flavour of the dressing comes from whole dried red chillies that are roasted until they become smoky and paprika-like.

Serves 4–6

200 g prawns
1 whole head of garlic
15 white peppercorns
vegetable oil, for frying and deep-frying
15 g plain flour

15 g cornflour
1 teaspoon ground white pepper
1 teaspoon ground sea salt
bunch of coriander

for the Roast Chilli Dressing:
3 dried chillies
vegetable oil, for frying
2 tablespoons freshly squeezed lime juice
1 teaspoon palm sugar
1 teaspoon fish sauce

1 Shell the prawns, leaving their heads on. Run a knife along the back to remove any dark intestinal veins.
2 Make the dressing: remove the seeds from the dried red chillies. Heat a little vegetable oil in a pan and very slowly roast the chillies until browned and fragrant. Leave to cool. Pound the roasted chillies in a mortar with a pestle. Transfer to a bowl and add the lime juice, palm sugar, fish sauce and 3 tablespoons of water. Set aside.
3 Pound the whole garlic, leaving the skin on, with the peppercorns.

4 Heat a little vegetable oil and put in the peppered garlic. Fry gently until the garlic is golden-brown, then drain on kitchen paper and leave to cool.

5 Mix the two flours with the ground pepper and the salt, and use this to dust the prawns.

6 Heat some more oil in a wok and deep-fry the prawns until just coloured and cooked through, around 2 minutes.

7 Drain and put in a serving bowl. Add the garlic and coriander, and toss everything together. Serve the chilli dressing separately.

Spicy

Spiced Potato Cakes

The whole complex tapestry of Indian spicing is very different from the flavouring in other Asian food. While I am always more drawn to the fresh zingy flavours of chillies and lime leaves and Thai basil, there are also times when I like to play around with Indian spices like cardamom and cumin.

These potato cakes are a really simple but smart (completely vegan) version of Indian street-food snacks. I serve them in bowls, with chickpeas.

200 g chickpeas
100 ml vegetable oil, plus more for frying
　　the potato cakes
2 teaspoons mustard seeds
2 teaspoons chilli powder
6 tomatoes, chopped
4 really big baking potatoes
4 red chillies, deseeded and finely
　　chopped
good handful of coriander leaves,
　　coarsely chopped, plus more for
　　garnish
salt and pepper
flour, for dusting

for the garam masala:
1 cinnamon stick
2 whole cloves
1 teaspoon cumin seeds
1 teaspoon black peppercorns
4 cardamom pods
½ teaspoon freshly grated nutmeg

The day before:
1 Put the chickpeas in cold water to soak overnight.

Next day:
2 Preheat the oven to 200°C/400°F/gas 6. Heat 100 ml of the vegetable oil in a large pan until smoking. Add the mustard seeds and sizzle for 30 seconds, then add the chilli powder and cook for a few moments longer until aromatic, stirring constantly to avoid burning.
3 Drain the chickpeas, keeping the soaking liquor. Add the chickpeas to the pan, with the tomatoes and half the soaking liquor, and bring to the boil. Cook for about 30

minutes, until the chickpeas are just soft. Season and
keep set aside.
4 While the chickpeas are cooking, bake the big
potatoes in their skins for 20–40 minutes, until they are
just cooked in the centre but are still holding together
nicely. Leave them to cool, then peel them and grate
them coarsely.
5 To make the garam masala: roast all the spices in a
dry pan until they release their aromas, then grind to a
fine powder in a coffee grinder or food processor.
6 Put one-third of the potato in a bowl and mix with the
chillies, coriander and a heaped teaspoon of garam
masala. Season with a little salt.

7 Divide the seasoned potato mix into 4 pieces and roll
these into balls, then work the remaining potato into 4
pieces. Flour your hands, flatten one of these pieces
into a large round in your palm. Place a ball of
seasoned potato in the middle and mould the flattened
plain potato around it to enclose it completely. Flatten
out into a cake shape, repeat until all the mix is used
and put in the fridge for an hour to firm up.
8 Dust the potato cakes with seasoned flour and fry in
hot oil for a few minutes on each side, until dark
golden-brown.
9 Serve with the chickpeas, heated through again if
necessary, and sprinkled with coriander.

Spicy

Naan Bread

My wife, Angie, introduced me to Indian food in the days when we had just met and had no money. She used to cook a big *dhal* and we would go to the local take-away and buy *naan* bread to have with it. Nowadays I make my own.

500 g plain flour
1 teaspoon salt
1 teaspoon sugar
1 teaspoon fresh yeast
100 ml milk
150 ml natural yoghurt
60 g clarified butter or ghee

1 Put the flour, salt, sugar and yeast in a large bowl and mix well.
2 Heat the milk until lukewarm.
3 Reserving 1 tablespoon of the yoghurt, add the rest to the milk, blending thoroughly.
4 Melt the butter and add to the milk and yoghurt, mixing well.
5 Pour slowly over the flour and mix together, then knead until you have a springy dough.
6 Leave the dough to rise in a warm place for about 1 hour, until doubled in size.
7 Divide the dough into 10 even-sized balls, cover and leave for 15 minutes.
8 Preheat a moderate grill and put a large baking tray under it to heat for about 10 minutes.
9 Flatten the balls of dough into rough teardrop shapes and spread with the reserved yoghurt.
10 Place on the hot baking tray and grill under a moderate heat for about 2–3 minutes on each side until golden. Watch all the time, as they can change colour and burn very quickly.

Spiced Lentils

These are wonderful with seared scallops.

50 g red lentils
vegetable oil
1 teaspoon cardamom seeds, crushed
1 small red onion, chopped
10 g root ginger, peeled, smashed
   then chopped
1 garlic clove, crushed
1 long red chilli, chopped
2 large ripe plum tomatoes
salt
300 ml chicken stock
bunch of coriander leaves
50 g butter
1 teaspoon crème fraîche
juice of ½ lemon

The day before:
1 Soak the lentils in cold water overnight.

Next day:
2 Drain off excess water from the lentils, cover with fresh water, bring to the boil and simmer until just tender. Take off the heat and set aside.
3 Heat some vegetable oil in a pan, add the cardamom seeds and cook for a few seconds. Add the onion, ginger, garlic, chilli, tomatoes and salt, and cook for 4–5 minutes.
4 Add the contents of the lentil pan and the stock, and cook for a further 3–4 minutes.
5 Take one-third of the mixture and blitz it to a purée in a blender. Return this to the pan and add the coriander leaves, butter, crème fraîche and lemon juice. Bring back to the boil, then serve immediately.

Along with the lentils, ✳ **Spinach with Chilli and Yoghurt** is another dish that can happily accompany Western ingredients like seared fish or lamb. Heat 40 g ghee or clarified butter in a heavy pan and cook a diced large onion gently until golden. Add 1 teaspoon each ground coriander and ground cumin, ½ teaspoon each turmeric and mustard seeds, and about ¼ teaspoon chilli powder. Mix well and cook for a minute or two until aromatic. Add 450 g washed spinach, with a little water if the mixture seems too dry. Cover and leave off the heat for the spinach to steam for 5 minutes. Transfer half to a blender, add a tablespoon of yoghurt and purée. Stir into the pan, to give a nice combination of smooth and chunky. Heat through briefly, then serve with more yoghurt spooned on top. Finish by thinly slicing a long red chilli and scattering it over.

69

Spicy

Desserts

After a spicy meal, frankly all I want to eat is some fresh fruit, like mango, with some raspberries or strawberries in season and a freshly sliced pineapple, and perhaps some refreshing jelly, water ice or sorbet.

One of the simplest sorbets to make is ✳**Fresh Lychee and Ginger Sorbet**. First make a stock syrup by boiling up 250 ml water with 250 g caster sugar, then take this off the heat as soon as the sugar dissolves. Purée 300 g of peeled, stoned lychees with the syrup. Add 50 g grated root ginger, leave to cool, then churn in an ice-cream maker, according to manufacturer's instructions.

Be really decadent and pour a bottle of pink champagne into a tray and freeze until set, then smash into large pieces and serve with a big plate of fresh fruit.

Lime Water Ice
Makes 1 tray

125 ml lime juice (about 4–6 limes)

for the stock syrup:
125 g sugar
1½ tablespoons lemon juice
1 vanilla pod
1 cinnamon stick

1 First make the stock syrup: put all ingredients in a large pot with 500 ml water, bring to the boil and stir well. Remove from heat and let cool slightly.
2 Mix in the lime juice. Let cool completely, take out the cinnamon and vanilla, pour into an ice tray and freeze.

Mint Jelly

2 small bunches of mint
250 g caster sugar
3 tablespoons lemon juice
2 leaves of gelatine

1 Chop one of the bunches of mint.
2 Put the sugar in a pan with 100 ml water. Bring to the boil and add the rest of the mint. Off the heat, leave to infuse

for 30 minutes. Add the lemon juice.
3 Put the gelatine leaves in a bowl of cold water to rehydrate, then squeeze out excess water.
3 Strain the mint syrup and, while still warm, add the gelatine and stir to dissolve, then mix in the chopped mint.
4 Chill for about 12 hours until set.

Coconut Jelly
You can buy fresh coconut juice (found inside young coconuts) in supermarkets.

Makes 1 big tray

500 ml coconut milk
5 leaves of gelatine
150 ml young coconut juice

1 Bring the coconut milk to the boil with 100 ml water. Skim and take off the heat.
2 Put the gelatine in some cold water to rehydrate, then squeeze out excess.
3 Pour the hot liquid over the gelatine, stirring all the time until well mixed, then leave to cool.
4 When cooled, mix in the coconut juice. Pour into a deep tray or dish and leave to set in the fridge.
5 Cut into cubes and serve with fresh fruit.

Comfort

It has nothing to do with season; or has it? It has more to do with texture than flavour; or has it? What is comfort food? What is it that makes me suddenly yearn to eat a great big meat pie, or fishcakes, or bubble and squeak? What makes a bowl of duck noodle soup warming, but not comforting in quite the same way as mashed potato with spring onions, or creamy polenta or potato gnocchi with piping-hot Bolognese sauce and lots of parmesan cheese are comforting.

Comfort food is quite indulgent, almost decadent in its own way; the stuff that, as grown-ups, you feel you are not really supposed to have, but that gives you a sense of security and well-being. It is connected with memories of supper dishes made out of leftovers that you had on a Sunday evening when you were a child, or eating fish and chips somewhere warm on an icy day. I remember huddling with Angie inside a kids' playhouse in an adventure playground in Australia while it was raining outside, eating potato cakes we had bought – thick slices of potato dipped in batter and deep-fried. Comfort food is big, dense and childish, and I think that this is what it is really all about, the association with childhood, growing up and feeling secure.

I have two clear childhood memories of kitchens. I can still smell the incredible aromas that used to fill my uncle's mother's kitchen in Australia. She is white Russian and cooks the most incredible pork and onion dumplings, wrapped in dough and boiled, and dishes like stuffed cabbage and stuffed peppers.

My strongest memories, though, are all of my grandmother's kitchen in Maitland. I was born in Sydney, then we moved to Melbourne – where my father had an orange juice factory – when I was four. Just as he started to be successful, my mum died and my two brothers and I moved up to Maitland to live with my grandmother, or

71

Nanna as she was always known. In wintertime it was quite cold and we had open fires and flannelette sheets and big blankets, but we were very nurtured.

My grandmother used to bake and cook all the time. In the morning there were big bowls of porridge, with soft brown sugar that melted around the rim, though I could never eat the milk that was poured around the edge, because of an allergy to raw milk. In the evenings after school we would have big bowls of vegetable soup with dumplings or grilled lamb chops with long tails and fat that was really crispy, with lots of mashed potato. Most nights there was mash, often with onions, or it would be turned into bubble and squeak, with anything from cabbage to Brussels sprouts, parsnips, carrots and onions, chopped-up ham, and always fried eggs on top.

There was one dish I remember, asparagus mornay, that contradicts most of what I believe about cooking, because it was made with tinned asparagus, but it was so good – and it was serious comfort food. The asparagus was mixed with chopped hard-boiled eggs, covered in white sauce, then fresh breadcrumbs and grated cheese, and baked in the oven.

The kitchen was the heart of my grandmother's house. It was massive. There was a couch with wooden arms and huge puffy cushions, and at the other end a big dining table. It was also the engine room, because to heat the water and the house – and keep us in food – we had to cut wood and then light the big enamelled combustion stove, which was always on the go by six in the morning. That stove was beautiful, a really butch piece of machinery that stirred and steamed and hissed. I have wanted a combustion stove like that ever since.

Because it was going all the time, there were always joints of meat being cooked, or a chicken, and lots of roast vegetables, biscuits and cakes and puddings, like gramma pie, made with the gramma pumpkin, a sweet version of the blue pumpkin but a lot bigger, which was cooked with sugar and cinnamon. And there was always a caramel slice in the fridge.

The kitchen seemed to be the natural place for me to be. It was where things happened, where my father talked to my grandmother while she cooked or where he made soup with pearl barley when he came up at the weekends. It was a special place. On Christmas Day, even when she was nearly seventy, my grandmother would still cook a feast for about twenty-five people on that combustion stove: roast lamb, pork, turkey, chicken, a whole ham, and about seven vegetables – parsnips, carrots, onions, potatoes, pumpkin, etc. The adults would eat inside and the kids used to have a table set up in the big covered veranda attached to the kitchen, what Australians call a tacky-on-the-backy.

It was my job to make the chicken gravy, the way she showed me – by taking the bird out of its roasting dish, putting the tray on top of the stove and sprinkling in some flour, which would get brown and roasted, then adding water and boiling it up until it was thick and tasty with the chicken juices. I used to get paid a dollar to wash up, but I was happy doing it, because I liked the social thing about being in the kitchen, listening to the gossip. For me a kitchen should always be a place where the family lives, and talks and cooks.

'You can win a lot of hearts by simply roasting a corn-fed chicken, rubbed with olive oil and sprinkled with sea salt, stuffed with a lemon, more sea salt and a couple of bay leaves'

I still think you can win a lot of hearts by simply roasting a corn-fed chicken, its skin rubbed with olive oil and sprinkled with sea salt, stuffed with a lemon, some more sea salt and a couple of bay leaves, then serving it with roast pumpkin – either the big gold pumpkin or butternut squash, not the Halloween pumpkin, which I call spaghetti veg and which isn't solid enough to hold its form and flavour. I cut it into wedges, pour a little olive oil over it, put in lots of sprigs of garden rosemary and roast it for about three-quarters of an hour.

A great roast is true comfort food – chicken, lamb, beef or shoulder of pork, its skin smeared with vinegar, left to dry, then salted so that it crisps up gorgeously before being seared then roasted on a trivet over a roasting pan with some water in the base, to keep the moisture in and give good juices for the gravy.

The day I realized that my grandmother was going downhill was when we turned up to visit after we had grown up and I had moved back to Melbourne. The stove hadn't been lit and there was very little in the fridge. She had lived by herself for such a long time, she had lost that feeling for cooking every day of her life.

When we were kids we didn't really realize how good it was living there. My grandmother had chicken sheds and a garden full of herbs and vine tomatoes that made the best sandwiches in thick bread with salt and pepper. Down the side of the house there were peach trees laden with fruit, passion fruit vines, lemon trees, orange trees, and sugar bananas that we just let the birds eat. Jump the fence and there were 200-year-old mulberry trees. We grew rhubarb and that was another of the dishes she taught me to cook properly, never with water, just with sugar sprinkled on top, covered with foil and put into a slow oven until sweet and soft. I do the same thing now with apples.

I guess my cooking is very different from my grandmother's in many ways, but I still don't think you can beat a good roast chicken, or great mash, and when I make something like a big tajine with masses of couscous, although it might be a dish she would never even have heard of, I think that the sense of cooking and sharing plenty of food with friends and family is something she would have heartily approved of.

Comfort

Guinea Fowl Tajine with Couscous and Harissa

I really hope that no one who tries this dish portions it up neatly in the kitchen and then takes it to the table, or packs the couscous into little ring moulds and serves slivers of guinea fowl balanced on top. This is wonderful, honest, stick-the-pot-in-the-middle-of-the-table food. It's the kind of dish that you eat over several hours on a Sunday afternoon, and when you are still around the table drinking coffee and friends turn up you say, 'Pick up a plate and join us.' That's great, I love that feeling of generous food.

The exciting thing about cooking in a tajine is that you absolutely mustn't take the lid off until everyone is sitting around the table ready to eat. Keep telling yourself, 'It's going to be all right', then open it up and, when everyone gasps as the aromas burst out from the meat and vegetables and the rich gelatinous juices, you'll feel the real joy of achievement. I never believe cooks who say they don't need applause. Let's be honest, we're all egotists at heart; we want people to smile and say, 'Fantastic, delicious, that was great!'

Certain pots and pans are just designed to do a specific job, like a well-seasoned omelette pan, or a wok – don't let anyone tell you that you can stir-fry as well in a frying pan – and a terracotta tajine is a great piece of design. The base gives you a good big surface area with which to work, so you can put in whole birds, like these guinea fowl, a plump chicken, or a quartet of pigeons; or you can pack in shanks of

lamb, with their bones sticking upwards, crossed over to look like a tepee. If you don't have a tajine, of course, any good large heavy pan with a tight-fitting lid will work almost as well.

The original tajines were cooked in pits, dug in the ground and lined with coals. You put in your tajine, leaving the bulbous top sticking out (perhaps to remind you where you had buried it!), then you packed sand around it, which would get red-hot in the sun and enable the meat and vegetables inside to cook away slowly. These days you can buy tajines that can be started off on the hob, but I prefer to brown the meat first in a pan, then transfer it to a clean tajine for putting in the oven.

Making a tajine begins with a relaxing afternoon in the kitchen the day before you want to eat it, cooking up *harissa*, the hot sauce that will be served with it, and mixing *chermoula*, a spicy marinade for the meat or fowl. They are sweet-sounding words, aren't they – *harissa*, *chermoula*, tajine, couscous? They have a kind of singing, dreamy ring about them that I associate with good times.

The *chermoula* – made with garlic, onions, ginger, lemon juice, honey, coriander and parsley – curiously also has fish sauce in it, which the North Africans must have originally used as a substitute for salt.

To make the ✳ **Harissa** you first need to roast 30 g each of coriander, cumin and fennel seeds together in a dry frying pan that you have already got good and hot on the hob. Drop the spices in, then turn off the heat and keep stirring until the spices colour and the aromas really come out. Once roasted, grind them in a mortar and pestle or an electric grinder until fine.

Next, heat 200 ml olive oil in a heavy-bottomed pan, add 3 large chopped red onions and 8 chopped garlic cloves, then cook gently until softened. Add the freshly ground spices and let them cook through for a few more minutes. Then add 4 deseeded and chopped red peppers and 20 deseeded and chopped long red (serrano) chillies (less if you don't like it as hot as I do) and cook for 10–15 minutes. Put the sauce through a blender until it is churned to a paste, then return it to the stove and let it cook out for at least 20 minutes, better still up to an hour, until the *harissa* darkens from a yellowy colour to a rich dark red. When it is ready you will see little bubbling volcanic craters breaking the surface of the sauce, where the oil will start to ooze through. Take it off the heat and let it cool down. The *harissa* can be kept in the fridge for up to two weeks, provided you cover the surface with a thin layer of olive oil.

The other accompaniment for the tajine is ✳ **Couscous**. I used to go through the whole ritual of steaming the little semolina grains in muslin, taking them out, fluffing them up and steaming them again, sometimes with saffron. There is a kind of romance about having the muslin that you use only for couscous hanging up in the kitchen, together with the special straining cloth you use for jam and all that stuff. These days, though, I unashamedly make the couscous the lazy way using pre-prepared grains. I put them in a bowl, with some sultanas scattered over the top and some big pieces of butter, then I pour boiling water over the top, cover the bowl and leave it to cook itself, while I open a bottle of wine.

'They are sweet-sounding words, aren't they – *harissa*, *chermoula*, tajine, couscous? They have a kind of singing, dreamy ring about them that I associate with good times'

Guinea Fowl Tajine with Couscous and Harissa (continued)

You can use this recipe for whole chicken, or lamb shanks, but increase the cooking time to 3 hours; for pigeon, reduce it to 1 hour. In each case, lower the temperature halfway through.

2 oven-ready guinea fowl
a little olive oil
3 carrots, cut into chunks
3 red onions, cut into chunks
about 12 dried prunes, dates or figs
2 Preserved Lemons (see page 23)
2 sprigs of mint, for garnish
small jar of harissa, bought or home-
    made (see page 75), to serve

for the chermoula:
2 large red onions, roughly chopped
3 garlic cloves
3.5-cm piece of fresh root ginger,
    roughly chopped
200 ml olive oil
200 ml lemon juice (about 3 lemons)
1 tablespoon Thai fish sauce
1 generous tablespoon honey
1 tablespoon ground cumin
1 tablespoon ground paprika
1 tablespoon ground turmeric
1 teaspoon hot chilli powder
large handful of flat-leaf parsley
large handful of coriander

for the couscous:
200 g ready-prepared couscous
1 teaspoon salt
20 g butter
small handful of sultanas

The day before:
1 To make the chermoula: roast the spices until aromatic. Put them with all the other chermoula ingredients in a blender and process to a smooth paste.
2 Pour over the guinea fowl and leave in the fridge to marinate overnight.

Next day:
3 Preheat the oven to 220°C/425°F/gas 7.
4 Heat a little olive oil in a large frying pan and brown the guinea fowl quickly on all sides.
5 Put the carrots, onions and fruit into the tajine and place the guinea fowl on top. Pour in around 400 ml water, to come about 1 cm from the top of the tajine base.
6 Cover the tajine with its lid and cook in the oven for about 45 minutes, then turn the oven setting down to 180°C/350°F/gas 4 and cook for another 45 minutes.
7 About 15 minutes before serving, prepare the couscous: rinse it in cold water and put into a large bowl. Season with salt. Cut the butter into chunks and scatter on top. Scatter the sultanas around the edge of the bowl. Pour boiling water over the top to cover by about 1 cm. Place a plate over the top and leave for about 10 minutes until the grains have plumped up and become tender.
8 Meanwhile, pare off the peel from the preserved lemons and cut it into thin strips. Chop the mint.
9 Open up the tajine at the table and scatter with the preserved lemon strips and chopped mint. Serve the couscous and harissa separately.

Comfort

Potatoes are probably the first ingredients that spring to mind when I think of comfort food, perhaps because of those associations with childhood. When you need something easy and cheerful, a big bowl of ✳**Leek and Potato Soup** is so right. The whole of the onion family has a great affinity with potatoes, in the same way that tomato and basil are natural partners. You might as well make a soup like this in large quantities, and keep some in the fridge (for a few days) so that you can just reheat it for lunch or supper.

To make about 5 litres, sweat roughly 500 g chopped onions in about 125 g butter until they soften but don't colour, then add 4 crushed garlic cloves, 4 chopped celery stalks and a bay leaf, and cook for about 4 minutes. Season and add the chopped white sections of 2 large leeks (keep greens for later) and 1.25 kg peeled and roughly chopped potatoes. Cook for 4 more minutes, season again, then add 4 litres of vegetable stock. Bring it to the boil, skimming the surface, then turn the heat down to a simmer. Throw in the chopped leek greens and cook for about 8 minutes. Right at the end, pour in 125 ml double cream, bring the soup back to the boil and immediately take the pan off the heat. If you want a smooth soup you can purée it, or part of it, otherwise leave it as it is. Either way, just check the seasoning.

Most cultures have potato recipes that have kept people going in times when maybe there was little else to eat. In the north of Italy, around Piedmont, potato gnocchi with fontina cheese is one of the traditional dishes.

Potato Gnocchi with Fontina

Serves 4–6

1 kg floury potatoes
salt and freshly ground black pepper
500 g flour
200 g fontina cheese, sliced
50 g grated parmesan cheese
3 tablespoons double cream

1 Peel the potatoes and boil in as little water as possible until just tender. Drain very thoroughly, and put back in the pan over a low heat for a few minutes, so they are as dry as possible.
2 Preheat the oven to 200°C/400°F/gas 6.
3 Mash the potatoes while still warm (they must be warm for this to work). Season, then slowly add the flour, kneading gently by folding the edges of the mixture into the centre and pressing down lightly before sprinkling in each further addition of flour, until it is soft and 'duvet-like'. Don't overwork or you will spoil the structure of the dough and end up with gnocchi that are powdery on the outside and pulpy inside.
4 Take little balls of the dough and roll into sausage shapes about 2 cm across. Cut each of these into 3-cm pieces.
5 Press each piece of dough against the back of a fork, so that it curves slightly and the prongs leave indentations, which will help the gnocchi hold their accompanying sauce.
6 Cook in plenty of lightly salted simmering water for 3–4 minutes. The gnocchi are done 2 minutes after they rise to the surface.
7 Arrange the gnocchi in a buttered dish. Sprinkle with a layer of fontina and

a little grated parmesan. Pour over the cream, then season with black pepper. Repeat again, finishing with a layer of freshly grated parmesan.

8 Place in the oven for 10–15 minutes. Remove and sprinkle with black pepper and a little more freshly grated parmesan to serve.

The other great gnocchi dish is ✳ **Gnocchi with Bolognese Sauce**. Bolognese was one of the first dishes I was taught to cook, at about ten years old, on a special cooking day at school. That was when I learned that you must fry the onions before the garlic, otherwise the garlic will burn.

For 4–6 people you need about 3–4 chopped onions, 10 smashed garlic cloves – it's got to be garlicky – and about 200 ml olive oil. Heat the oil and sweat the onions until they are clear, then put in the garlic and cook for another minute or so. Stir in at least 1 kg minced beef, pour in a cupful of water and a couple of tinfuls of plum tomatoes (it's really only worth using fresh tomatoes when they are fantastically ripe and sweet), a little tomato paste, some bay leaves, fresh oregano, salt and pepper, and let it bubble away for about 2½ hours, until it is thick and delicious.

Pour it over your cooked gnocchi and grate a whole load of parmesan cheese over the top. If you prefer a rich ✳ **Tomato Sauce**, make it in exactly the same way, but without the beef – you can add a pinch of cumin to the onions if you like – cooking it slowly for a couple of hours, then stirring in a good tablespoon of extra-virgin olive oil, plenty of freshly chopped basil, salt and pepper and a squeeze of lemon juice.

Mash The ultimate comfort food must surely be ✳ **Mashed Potato**. I think really good mash has to be piping hot, and beaten and worked quite hard until it is creamy and peaky but still has the texture of a good floury potato. If you can, use potatoes still covered in protective earth and quite fresh out of the ground, because as potatoes get older the starch begins to break down and turns into sugar, so that you end up with a sweetish, more cornflour-textured, sloppy mash.

You can't really make hard-and-fast rules about the ratio of liquid or butter to potato; you need to take a look at the texture of your cooked potato and feel your way. If I am cooking, say, 2 kg of potatoes – I like powdery red ones – I may well use about 8 tablespoons of milk and 80 g butter, but I'll start with a little of each and add more, depending on how much the potato takes up.

I cook the potatoes first with a good half-handful of Maldon salt, drain them, then put them back in the hot pan over a very low flame for a minute or so, to steam off the excess moisture. Then I add some of the milk and seasoning – lots of salt and white pepper, which I think, for some reason, works slightly better than black pepper with mash. Then I start beating and, when the milk is hot, I add some of the butter so that it melts quickly. Now you just have to beat and work the potato, still on the hob, adding more milk and butter as you like, until the mixture becomes volcanic and starts erupting into bubbles. If you want to add a touch of cream, fine.

'The ultimate comfort food must surely be mashed potato'

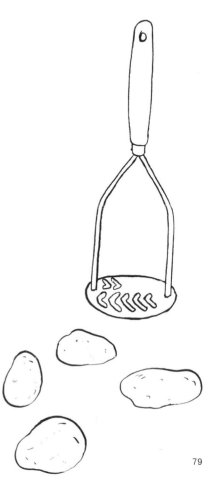

'Just leave the scallops be, don't worry about them; when they want to come away from the pan, after about a minute, they will do it naturally'

I sometimes get yearnings for mash with a piece of roast cod or some ✳**Scallops with Black Butter and Thyme**. You have to have absolutely fresh scallops, not frozen, and they have to be beautifully seared, so that you get that slight crispiness against the softness of the mash. When cooking scallops, first season them, then get a frying pan really, really hot, with no oil – which would just turn black and smoke and leave a nasty mark around the edge of the scallops. Put a little olive oil on a plate, drop the scallops in it and smear it thinly all over them. Put them in the pan, and don't even think about trying to shake it. Just leave the scallops be, don't worry about them; when they want to come away from the pan, after about a minute, they will do it naturally. At that point, flip them over, give them about 30 seconds, then take the pan off the heat, drop in a couple of big knobs of butter, let it bubble and go dark, sprinkle in some thyme and a squeeze of lemon juice, then pile the scallops on top of some mash and pour the black butter over the top.

If you want to cook a piece of ✳**Roast Cod** to go with your mash, the same principles apply: hot pan – one that will transfer to the oven – oil and season the fish (leave the skin on, but make sure it is completely dry). Put it into the pan, skin side down, then leave it alone, without shaking, until, like a pancake, it just starts to brown around the outside. Pop it into the oven at 200°C/400°F/gas 6 for about 8 minutes, then take it out and leave it on top of the stove for about a minute. It will lift itself naturally from the bottom of the pan and you can put a palette knife underneath, flip it over and you will have lovely crispy skin on top. I can't think of much better comfort food than a piece of roast cod with some new-season's olive oil (see page 22) drizzled over, a twist of black pepper and a bowl of the Irish version of mashed potato, champ.

✳**Champ** is really sexy stuff. For enough to serve 4–6 people you need about 6 spring onions (scallions as they are called in Ireland and the USA) to a kilo of potatoes. Boil the potatoes in the usual way, and while they are cooking prepare the spring onions. The quickest way to peel them is to put them under very cold running water for a few moments. All the healthy bits of the onion will stiffen up because they take up the water, and the sad outside leaves will go limp and peel off easily. Chop the spring onions, separating the green from the white. The white part of the onion will be cooked slightly, the green thrown in at the end for freshness and crunch.

Traditionally champ is made with boiling milk, but I quite like to do it with cream, too. When the potatoes are almost done, bring about 100 ml double cream and 3 tablespoons milk to the boil in a pan with about 25 g butter, then add the chopped white part of the onions and simmer for a few minutes and season. Mash the potatoes and mix in the hot cream and milk and the chopped green part of the spring onions. Serve in big bowls with an extra knob of butter melting into it.

I've seen champ done in a posher way, with the cream mixture and the green part of the spring onions whizzed to a blindingly bright green paste before being mixed into the potato, but personally I wouldn't mess with it.

Not surprisingly for a nation that loves its potatoes, the Irish have devised many ways with them. The other famous dish is ✳**Colcannon**, this time made with mashed potato and cabbage. To 1 kilo of potatoes you need about 250 g cooked cabbage, well drained, seasoned and tossed in some butter. Mix the mashed potato and cabbage together quite lightly, with a generous amount of butter – about 50 g – and season again if you need to. You can serve it straight away or leave it to cool, form it into cakes and shallow-fry them on both sides until crisp and golden on the outside.

When colcannon is done this way it isn't that dissimilar to ✳**Bubble and Squeak**, though with bubble and squeak you can add as many leftover cooked vegetables or strips of cooked bacon or ham to the mash as you like – whatever you have to hand really, from Brussels sprouts to parsnips – then fry it all up in one piece in hot oil in a frying pan. If you want to stop it from breaking up when you turn it over, wait until the underside is really brown and crisp, put a plate over the top of the pan and flip the two over together so that the cake of bubble and squeak is sitting fried side upwards. Slide it back into the pan to cook the other side. When that has crisped up, turn it out again in the same way, then you can cut it up into wedges.

There are three other variations of mashed potato that I like to do: swede and potato mash, celeriac mash and saffron mash. ✳**Swede and Potato Mash** is very simple: just cook equal quantities of each vegetable with a quartered onion and quite a lot of seasoning, then mash with milk and butter. ✳**Celeriac Mash** is again made with equal quantities of potato and celeriac, but when you cook them use three parts milk to one part olive oil, with 2 garlic cloves and salt and pepper, instead of water. When you drain the vegetables, keep the liquid and add this bit by bit as you mash the vegetables. You may not need it all.

✳**Saffron Mash** is made in a similar fashion, but you need to use new or small waxy potatoes, because the potatoes are going to be crushed and left in rough chunks rather than mashed. Before you cook with saffron (which is the dried stamens of the saffron crocus), you should always put the strands into a dry pan that has been well heated, then take it off the heat and move the saffron around the pan so that it changes colour to a deep russet and releases its flavour. Put the potatoes into a pan with three parts milk to one part olive oil, a sprig of thyme, the saffron and salt and pepper, and cook until soft. Then drain, reserving the liquid again. With a fork, just break up the potatoes, rather than mash them, then add the liquid bit by bit, folding it in very gently, so that you keep the chunky texture of the potato. If you find the saffron tastes a little dry and powdery in the mouth – which it can sometimes – a tiny squeeze of lemon juice or a drop of vinegar will bring the full flavour back.

The idea of crushing potatoes rather than mashing them is also, I think, one of the secrets of good fishcakes. For me, three things can spoil fishcakes: either the potato is overworked, the fish is overcooked, so the cakes turn out quite dry, or there is too much potato. You need about 30 per cent potato to 70 per cent fish.

Comfort

Salmon and Cod Fishcakes

The way I like to prepare the fish for fishcakes is to cook it in its skin, by covering it in boiling water and leaving it undisturbed for about half an hour, so that it is still slightly translucent, and will pull apart naturally at its seams into lovely big shards, in the way that good chip-shop fish steaming inside its batter comes away in chunks when you break into it. I quite like the crunch of the barely cooked onions in this recipe but, if you prefer, you can sweat them very gently in a little oil before adding them. These fishcakes are good with spinach wilted in a pan with a little butter, then finished off with a sprinkling of olive oil, lemon juice and black pepper, and/or some Salsa Verde (see page 84).

Makes 12 good-sized cakes

600 g salmon fillet, skin on
600 g cod fillet, skin on
boiling water
salt and freshly ground black pepper
dash of white wine vinegar
4 big floury baking-sized potatoes
2 medium red onions, very finely diced
3 long red (serrano) chillies, deseeded and chopped
2 good handfuls of chopped parsley (about 25 g)
2 good handfuls chopped coriander (about 25 g)
juice of 2 lemons and zest of 1
flour, for dusting
100 g butter
200 ml oil

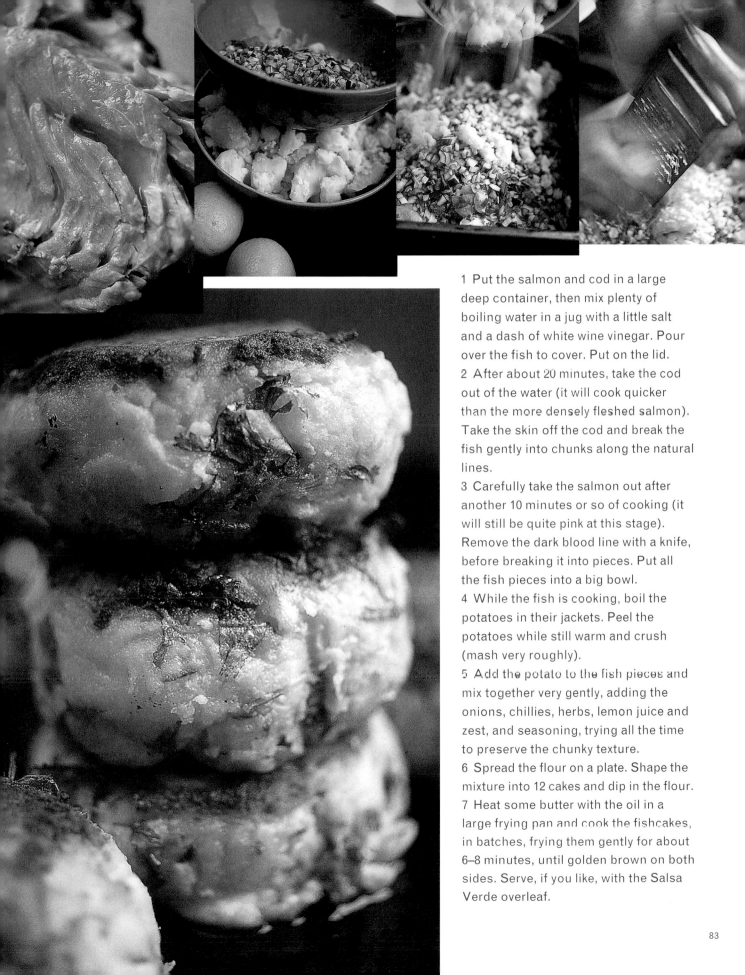

1 Put the salmon and cod in a large deep container, then mix plenty of boiling water in a jug with a little salt and a dash of white wine vinegar. Pour over the fish to cover. Put on the lid.

2 After about 20 minutes, take the cod out of the water (it will cook quicker than the more densely fleshed salmon). Take the skin off the cod and break the fish gently into chunks along the natural lines.

3 Carefully take the salmon out after another 10 minutes or so of cooking (it will still be quite pink at this stage). Remove the dark blood line with a knife, before breaking it into pieces. Put all the fish pieces into a big bowl.

4 While the fish is cooking, boil the potatoes in their jackets. Peel the potatoes while still warm and crush (mash very roughly).

5 Add the potato to the fish pieces and mix together very gently, adding the onions, chillies, herbs, lemon juice and zest, and seasoning, trying all the time to preserve the chunky texture.

6 Spread the flour on a plate. Shape the mixture into 12 cakes and dip in the flour.

7 Heat some butter with the oil in a large frying pan and cook the fishcakes, in batches, frying them gently for about 6–8 minutes, until golden brown on both sides. Serve, if you like, with the Salsa Verde overleaf.

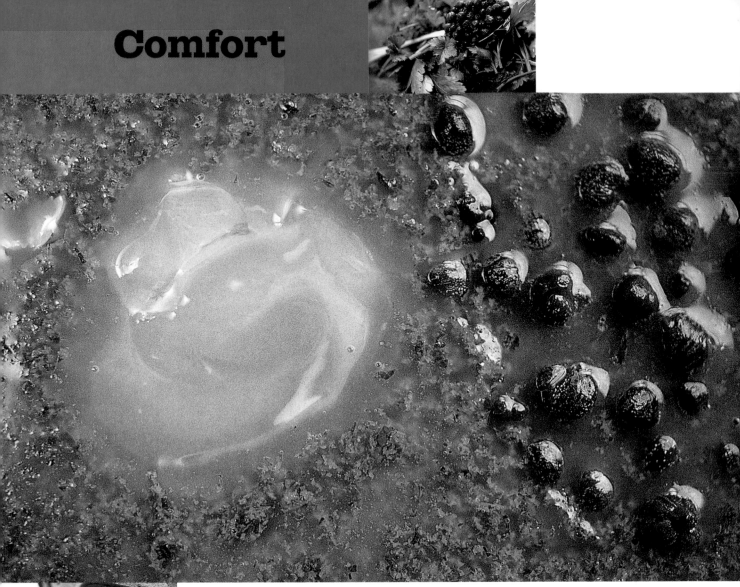

Comfort

Salsa Verde

Salsa Verde, which I like to serve with the Salmon and Cod Fishcakes on the previous page, is quite beautiful stuff, a sharp green sauce to spoon over the fishcakes or roast fish, or to cut through the richness of a dish like Bollito Misto (see page113). I think the secret of this and many blended sauces in other cultures, like Thai curry paste or Italian pesto, is to add your ingredients one by one, so that they are pounded to varying degrees, letting you really taste the individual flavours working together. If you blitz everything in one go, you end up with something much more homogeneous but less interesting. The soft-boiled eggs and the breadcrumbs bind everything together really creamily, but if worried about soft-boiled eggs, then cook them a little longer and mash up the yolks.

50 g white breadcrumbs
1½ tablespoons red wine vinegar
small bunch of basil
small bunch of flat-leaved parsley
3 garlic cloves, chopped
½ teaspoon salt and some freshly
    ground black pepper
120 ml olive oil
6 anchovy fillets, roughly chopped
1 tablespoon salted capers, rinsed
2 eggs

1 Soak the breadcrumbs in the vinegar briefly, then put into a food processor with the herbs, garlic and seasoning. Process briefly to a coarse paste.
2 With the motor running, add the olive oil a little at a time, until it is all incorporated.
3 Add the anchovies and capers and blitz for 2 seconds (literally press the switch on and off, to preserve the texture).
4 Bring a pan of water to the boil, put in the eggs and boil for 3 minutes. Run some cold water over the eggs briefly, then shell them while still warm. Scoop out the yolks and stir into your mixture. Finally chop the egg whites and fold them into the sauce.

Deep-fried Hake with Chips and Mushy Peas

If ever there was a food that felt naughty but comforting it has to be fish and chips. Go to a good fish and chip shop and you see people from all walks of life tucking in happily together. All the pretentiousness that sometimes goes with ordering food disappears in the face of sheer enjoyment. In Australia we used to get fish with potato cakes – slices of potato that had been floured and battered, then deep-fried.

I like to make fish and chips with hake, which is a fish that must be eaten as soon as possible when you get it home. All fish should ideally be eaten on the day you buy it, but hake in particular quickly turns white and chalky, whereas you want it to be translucent. Because it doesn't have much of a body structure, it cooks really quickly. Never buy it frozen, as it will turn to pulp.

The mushy peas in this recipe are not marrowfat, like the ones you find in chip shops, but fresh peas puréed. The potatoes should be new-season's if possible, and still covered in dirt, which usually shows that they haven't been stored for a long time.

1 kg potatoes
4 skinless pieces of hake, each
  about 150 g

for the batter:
225 ml Newcastle Brown Ale
1 egg, lightly beaten
40 g fresh yeast or 20 g dried
200 g flour, plus more for dusting
pinch of salt

for the Mushy Peas:
250 g shelled garden peas
salt and pepper
20 g butter
½ teaspoon sugar

1 First make the batter: mix the beer, egg and yeast together until smooth (If using dried, first warm it with a little beer to dissolve it and add a pinch of sugar). Gradually beat in the flour until a creamy batter is formed. Season with salt and allow to rest for 45 minutes.
2 Prepare the Mushy Peas: cook the peas in boiling salted water, until just soft. Melt the butter and put into a food processor with the peas and sugar (or use a hand blender) and process to a rough purée. Adjust the seasoning if necessary and keep warm.
3 Peel the potatoes and cut into chunky chips of equal size. Leave in a bowl of cold water for 20 minutes to remove excess starch. Remove and dry well.

4 Heat the oil to 140°C in a deep-fat fryer or a large pan (making sure the oil comes no further than halfway up). The rough rule of thumb is 100 g of chips to a litre of oil so that the chips have plenty of room to move and the temperature of the oil will not fall too quickly when the chips are put in. So if your fryer isn't big enough, cook the chips in batches.
5 Preheat a hot grill. Put the chips carefully in the oil and cook for about 10 minutes, then remove from the oil and drain. This is the blanching stage which helps to remove the excess water from the potato so that in the final frying process the chips will crisp up properly.
6 Increase the temperature of the oil to 220°C and put the chips back in. Shake the pan so that they don't stick together and cook for about 6–8 minutes or until brown and crisp. Remove from the fryer and drain on kitchen paper in the grill pan. Sprinkle with salt and keep warm under the switched-off hot grill.
7 Lightly flour the hake, dip it into the batter, then deep-fry for 5–6 minutes. Drain and serve the fish with the chips and the peas.

Polenta In the north of Italy in years gone by, polenta probably played a similar role to potatoes in Ireland – it kept poor families going when times were tough. Now, like Champ and Colcannon, it still satisfies a need for comfort food, not only in Italy but in many other countries. In regions like the Veneto or Friuli, a bowl of polenta on the table is as natural a part of any meal as potatoes in northern Europe or rice in Asia.

This soft polenta, made with mascarpone cheese, is really creamy, but with a great texture – a kind of cross between mashed potato and white sauce, which goes brilliantly with meat dishes in particular. Don't try to grill it or fry it; it won't work. For that you need to make ✳**'Hard' Polenta**. Just follow the recipe, but don't add the cream or mascarpone, and add only a little grated parmesan at the end.

Grease something like a loaf tin (you can oil it, then line it with cling-film, if you prefer). Pour in the polenta and flatten off the surface. Leave the tin in the fridge for a couple of hours until the polenta has set and is good and cold, then turn it out, peel the cling-film off and cut the polenta into slices. Cut each slice into big wedgy chips, roll them in polenta flour, then deep-fry, just like potato chips.

In every culture there is superstition, even in cooking. With polenta they say you should stir it in one direction only; if you turn the spoon back the other way you let the evil spirits out. Whether you believe in evil spirits or not is up to you, but the message makes sense, because if you stir it one way it rolls nicely and stays smooth. If you roll it back again the other way it becomes lumpy. The other story is that Marie Antoinette used to keep polenta in her cleavage as an emergency food supply – you can take or leave that one too.

There is 100 g of polenta in this recipe, enough for 10 people, but I find it hard to make much less because you need the volume to get the air through the mixture properly. You can always keep any that is left over in the fridge, then reheat it (if you like you can do this with the bowl covered in punctured cling-film in the microwave) and serve it for supper with ham or sausages.

Serves 10

500 ml milk
2–3 garlic cloves, smashed with the
    blade of a knife
2 teaspoons salt
1 teaspoon freshly ground black pepper
100 g instant polenta flour
200 ml double cream
150 g mascarpone cheese
50 g grated parmesan cheese

1 In a jug, mix the milk with an equal volume of water.
2 Put half the milk and water mixture in a large saucepan with the garlic and the salt and pepper. Bring to the boil.

3 In a bowl, mix the rest of the milk and water with the polenta flour, leave for a few minutes to rehydrate, then add to the pan, stirring well until smooth.
4 Cook gently for 20 minutes, stirring regularly in the same direction, then add the cream and mascarpone and cook for another 10 minutes.
5 Just before serving, beat in the parmesan until it is completely mixed in. Adjust your seasoning if necessary. You may not need much more salt, as the parmesan will add its own saltiness.

'With polenta they say you should stir it in one direction only; if you turn the spoon back the other way you let the evil spirits out'

Comfort

Confit

Confit When I was learning how to cook at a restaurant called Jean Pierre in Melbourne, Tuesday morning was the day that the fresh ducks would come in. They would be roasted in the way that I still roast ducks, over water, and when they came out of the oven the wings would have fallen off into the mixture of duck fat and water at the bottom of the roasting trays. The meat was so soft and gelatinous it was wonderful, it fell away from the bones just like confit – the age-old way of cooking meat slowly in its own fat.

This recipe is for confit of rabbit, which I love flaked into pieces on top of slow-cooked beans, but you can do exactly the same thing with duck, chicken legs, guinea fowl or pheasant. Once you have your first tinful of fat, you can keep on boiling it up, skimming away the impurities that rise to the surface, then re-using it. Store it in jars in the fridge in between times.

Rabbit Confit

Serves 4–6 with the bean recipe that follows

6 cumin seeds
12 coriander seeds
100 g sea salt
small sprig of rosemary
3 juniper berries, crushed
6 garlic cloves, crushed
4 rabbit legs
about 500 g goose fat
2 bay leaves
1 teaspoon black peppercorns

The day before:
1 Put the cumin and coriander seeds in a dry pan and roast until they are slightly coloured and aromatic. Crush with the blade of a knife.
2 Mix with the salt, rosemary, juniper berries and garlic.
3 Rub the mixture over the rabbit legs and leave for 24 hours, turning twice.

Next day:
4 Preheat the oven to 190°C/375°F/gas 5.
5 Wipe the rabbit with kitchen paper and pat dry. Don't wash off the

marinade, because the science behind the process of confit is that the salt extracts the water from its cells, which will be reinflated with fat as the meat cooks gently. If you wash it, you will simply reinflate the cells with water, so the confit process won't work as well.
6 Cover with goose fat, add the bay leaves and peppercorns and cook for about 3 hours, or until the meat is almost falling away from the bone.

If you have the time to keep an eye on the oven, I find that raising the temperature to a peak and then reducing it slowly helps to keep those cells filled with fat, so you get extra-succulent meat. I start off the cooking process at 150°C/300°F/gas 2 for about 30 minutes, increase to 180°C/350°F/gas 4 for 15 minutes, up to 200°C/400°F/gas 6 for another 15 minutes, then 230°C/450°F/gas 8 for about 20 minutes. Check the fat is bubbling, then start to reduce the heat: 200°C/400°F/gas 6 for 30 minutes, 180°C/350°F/gas 4 for another 30 minutes, then switch off the oven and leave for 40 minutes or so, until the meat is falling off the bone.

Slow-cooked Beans

There is something about the texture of tinned beans that makes me shudder. As a child I could cope with tins of spaghetti, but baked beans no, and the same applies to any tinned beans – to me they are awful slimy things. Plump dried beans, however, especially those gorgeous big Spanish butter beans, slowly cooked until almost melting... now you're talking.

Serves about 4 as a side dish or served with confit of rabbit, more if turned into soup

200 g dried haricot beans or
   butter beans
100 ml olive oil
2 red onions, finely chopped

1 leek, finely chopped
1 carrot, finely chopped
3 garlic cloves, crushed
handful of thyme leaves
a few chopped sage leaves
5 tomatoes
100 g Swiss chard leaves, chopped
3 spring onions, chopped
salt and freshly ground black pepper
dash of red wine vinegar
handful of flat-leaved parsley,
   chopped
extra-virgin olive oil, to dress

for the bouquet garni:
1 carrot, cut in half lengthwise
1 leek
branch of sage
a few sprigs of thyme
1 celery stalk, cut in half lengthwise

The day before:
1 Soak the beans overnight in water.

Next day:
2 Heat the oil in a heavy pan and gently sweat the onions, leek, carrot, garlic and herbs until the vegetables are just soft.
3 Drain the beans of almost all their liquid and add them to the pan. Add enough water to cover. Don't add any seasoning as it will harden the skins of the beans.
4 Make the bouquet garni by tying the carrot, leek, sage, thyme and celery in a bundle with string and put in the pot.

5 Cook the beans at a gentle simmer for about 30 minutes. Don't boil the love out of them, as the Italians say!
6 Add the tomatoes and simmer very gently for about 2 hours, or until the beans are soft but still have a slight bite. You'll probably need to top up the water now and then, but the finished dish should have a slightly soupy consistency.
7 Add the chard and spring onions, season well and cook for 10-15 minutes.
8 Add the vinegar, which will cut through the richness of the sauce and, just before serving, sprinkle with parsley and a little extra-virgin olive oil.

I can quite happily eat platefuls of these beans, just as they are, with a big hunk of bread, or I serve them with roast fish, or add some chopped chorizo or a garlicky coarse sausage like Morteaux. To make ✳**Bean Soup**, add some stock or tomato passata (juice); if you want to thicken it, take out a few of the beans, purée them, then put them back into the pot. Beans cooked this way are also fantastic with petit sel, half-salted pork similar to a confit but not quite as fatty.

To make your own ✳**Petit Sel**, you need a kilo slab of good-quality quite lean belly pork. Cover heavily with salt and leave overnight, then next day don't wash off the salt, just put the pork into a big pot of cold water, bring to the boil and then cook quite gently for about 3½ hours. Leave it in the pot to cool down, otherwise if you try to lift it out it will fall apart. When it is cool, take the pork carefully from the pot and lay it on a tray in the fridge, cover with greaseproof paper and put something heavy on top to keep it flat.

The next day, cut the pork into big chunks, get a little oil very hot in a frying pan and put the pork in, skin side down, and leave for a good 10 minutes until you can see it colouring around the edges. Season with salt, then transfer to a hot oven and cook for about 10 minutes until you have a wonderful crispy surface and a gluey gelatinous texture to the meat. Serve it on top of a big bowl of beans, or with mash, or even with a bowl of Chinese noodles in some chicken stock, scattered with some chopped chillies and spring onions.

Another really nice idea to borrow from Asian cooking is to 'wash' some strips of skin from belly pork in some fish sauce, then hang them up in a warm place in the kitchen for 24 hours or so to dry (or put in the oven at the lowest possible setting for 3–4 hours), then deep-fry them. They turn an amazing red colour, and when they cool a little you can literally crumble them over the top of the beans with your fingers.

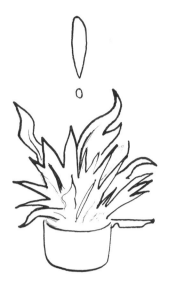

Chickpeas

Chickpeas are delicious cooked in the same way as for the bean recipe, but leave out the vinegar at the end. If you like, you can add more vegetables, such as pumpkin and potato, and spice up the pot with a little cumin and paprika. Serve the chickpeas with some Couscous (see page 75), *merguez*, or chunks of roast pork or chicken, and a bowl of Harissa (see page 75).

My whole family loves chickpeas, despite the fact that my wife has twice nearly set the house on fire cooking them. In Sydney, when we lived on the third floor, she put the chickpeas on, went out for the afternoon and completely forgot about them until she was close to home and saw the fire engines arriving and smoke billowing out of our window. Then, a few years later, we were living in Camden in London and she did exactly the same thing.

When we were in Sydney, though, she also used to work in a lovely little place called the Café l'Univers, where they rustled up some fantastic food. One dish I always remember was a beautiful ※ **Chicken Steamed on a Bed of Chickpeas, Tomato and Ginger**. I had never thought about the combination before, but they are really tasty if you braise your soaked chickpeas with 4 or 5 big, really ripe chopped tomatoes, a chopped onion and a good knuckle of chopped ginger, until everything reduces right down and all the flavours are really intense.

Braised Ox Cheek

In a restaurant you would use reduced veal jus for braising ox cheek, because you want something gelatinous to make the sauce thick and unctuous. The simplest way to get a similar effect is to put in a veal shin or even a pig's trotter. The trotter you can either discard after cooking, or take the bone out, roll the meat up in cling-film and leave it in the fridge for a while to firm up, then pan-fry and have it with some mash for a supper dish. The ox cheek is lovely with celeriac mash, scattered with a few chopped spring onions.

Serves 4-6

2 ox cheeks
salt and freshly ground black pepper
2 carrots
1 leek
3 celery stalks
bunch of flat-leaved parsley
small branch of sage
about 3 tablespoons olive oil
good-sized piece (about 125 g) of
    pancetta (rind and fat), cut into pieces
1 veal shin or pig's trotter
about ½ bottle of red wine

1 Preheat the oven to 190°/375°F/gas 5.
2 Season the ox cheeks really well. Tie the carrots, leek, celery and herbs tightly together in a bundle to make a bouquet garni.
3 Heat the oil in a big heavy pan, add the pancetta and ox cheeks and let them sit and sizzle. Don't shake the pan or try to flip over the ox cheeks too early, though you can move the pancetta around. Wait until the ox cheeks are well browned underneath and want to come away from the pan naturally before turning them over, as you want to get a good crust.

4 When both sides are nicely browned, add the bouquet garni and the veal shin or pig's trotter. Pour in the wine and boil it up to drive off the raw alcohol, then let it bubble away and reduce for about 10 minutes, scraping up the sticky caramelized bits of meat from the bottom of the pot.

5 Pour in about 1 litre of water, so that it almost covers the meat. Cover the top with a piece of baking paper and press this into the liquid to moisten it so that it won't burn.

6 Put in the oven and cook for about 3½ hours, until the liquid has reduced right down and the meat is so soft it virtually falls apart like confit. Change the paper once or twice during cooking, as it will absorb all the fat and impurities, leaving you with a lovely clear sauce.

Braised ox cheek makes a great filling for a chunky ✳**Suet Pudding**. Make up the suet dough with 350 g flour, 125 g butter, 125 g suet, a teaspoon of salt, ½ teaspoon of sugar, and a large tablespoon of warm water. Mix together, kneading lightly until you have a smooth dough, but try not to overwork it too much or the heat of your hands will melt the suet and the resulting pudding crust will be heavy rather than light and quite springy.

Roll out one-third of the dough into a circle large enough to cover the top of a 1.7-litre pudding basin and set side. Grease the inside of the bowl with plenty of butter, then cut out a round of greaseproof paper the right size to fit the bottom of the bowl, moisten it with water to make it more pliable and press inside. Roll out the larger piece of dough into a circle big enough to line the pudding basin, leaving a small overhang around the top and press in gently. Fill with the meat and its liquid. Put the suet dough lid on, bring the overhang over the top, moisten the underside with water and press gently to seal. Cover the top of the pudding with a double sheet of greaseproof paper, moistened with water, then tie with string and wrap the whole thing with foil.

Put into a large pan filled with boiling water to come three-quarters of the way up the side of the basin (put the basin on a folded tea towel to keep it away from the direct heat at the base of the pan). Put the lid on and simmer for about 4½ hours, topping up the water when necessary.

You could also bake the pudding in a bain-marie (or roasting tin half-filled with hot water) in the oven at about 180°C/350°F/gas 4 for about 4½–5hours, again sitting it on a folded tea towel, but I prefer the gentler all round bathing in steam that is produced from cooking it on top of the stove. Turn out and serve hot.

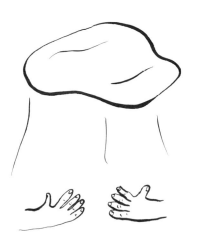

Puddings

The first time I tried making ✳**Sussex Pond Pudding** I was intrigued by the notion of a whole lemon steamed inside a suet pudding crust. It is such a wonderful idea. The secret is to use a really big fresh lemon with a thin rind. On that first occasion I made the pudding with a two-week-old lemon, which – though not visibly – would have been starting to dehydrate, changing the texture of the rind. The flavour was all there, but the lemon wasn't as melting as it should be. You must use unwaxed lemons, of course, or else you will have to scrub off the protective wax with hot water.

Spike the rind of the lemon all over with a fork, then line a small pudding basin with suet dough, using exactly the same method and half the quantities given for the pastry used with the ox cheek on the previous page. Put about 90 g of butter in the dough-lined basin, cover with 100 g caster sugar, then wedge the lemon upright into it, and cover with the same amount of sugar and another 90 g of butter. Put the top on the pudding and steam as described on the previous page – but for a little less time, about 2½ hours. During cooking, the sugar, lemon juice and butter all seep out into the suet crust.

You could make a similar pudding with an orange – perhaps a blood orange, so you get a lovely red colour, or even smaller individual puddings with limes in the centre.

Hot Vanilla Pudding with Toffee Sauce

This pudding is really decadent with ✳**Toffee Sauce**, which is actually more like a butterscotch sauce. Tip a cupful of caster sugar into a heavy pan and let it melt over a low heat, trying not to stir or disturb it. When it has melted, turn up the heat and let it bubble and turn into a dark caramel. At this point, whisk in 100 g butter, a bit at a time. It might bubble up a little, so be careful as hot caramel can burn you badly. Have 150 ml double cream ready and if the caramel starts to separate whisk some in quickly. Once the butter is all incorporated, gradually add all the cream, then bring to the boil and take off the heat.

To make a ✳**Chocolate Pudding**, use the same recipe but substitute 25 g of the flour with cocoa and serve with chocolate custard or toffee sauce.

100 g butter
100 g caster sugar
2 eggs
drop of vanilla extract
100 g flour
1 teaspoon baking powder
4 teaspoons milk

1 Preheat the oven to 180°C/350°F/gas 4.
2 Cream the butter and caster sugar together. Beat in the eggs a little at a time and then add the vanilla extract. Mix well.
3 Sift the flour and baking powder together and fold this into the egg and sugar mixture. Mix in the milk until smooth.
4 Grease a pudding basin with some butter, fill with the mixture and cover with foil.
5 Cook in a bain-marie (or roasting tin half-filled with hot water) in the oven for about 1 hour.

Comfort

Bramley Apple and Panettone Pudding

I like to make a great big pudding that lasts over several days, so people can stick a spoon in and have a piece with a cup of tea any time they feel like it.

Serve 8–10

500 ml double cream
500 ml milk
4 large eggs, plus 4 extra large yolks
100 g sugar
350 g Bramley apples
1 panettone, about 450 g
good handful of soft brown sugar

1 Preheat the oven to 190°C/375°F/gas 5.
2 Put the cream and milk in a large heavy-based pan and bring to the boil. Take off the heat.
3 In a bowl, beat the eggs, egg yolks and the sugar until the mixture is pale. Very slowly add the hot milk and double cream mixture and mix well, but don't whisk or you will thicken up the cream too much.
4 Peel the apples and slice them into chunks. Put in a large ovenproof dish. Cut the panettone into slices about 2 cm thick and lay them, overlapping slightly, on top of the apples. Scatter brown sugar to taste over the top, enough to make little clumps. Pour over the custard and leave to soak for about 10 minutes so that the panettone can absorb it.
5 Put the pudding in the oven for 18–20 minutes. When completely cooked it should be golden on top but still slightly wobbly to the touch.
6 Leave to set at room temperature for 15–20 minutes before serving.

Sticky Date Pudding

Serves 8

175 g dates, stoned and roughly chopped
1 teaspoon bicarbonate of soda
125 ml boiling water
50 g butter, plus more for greasing the moulds
175 g caster sugar, plus more for sprinkling
2 eggs, beaten
175 g flour
pinch of baking powder

1 Preheat the oven to 190°/375°/gas 5.
2 Put the dates in a bowl with the bicarbonate of soda and pour over the boiling water. Cover with cling-film and leave for about 20 minutes until the dates are soft. Leave to cool.
3 In a bowl, cream the butter and sugar until light and fluffy. Slowly add the beaten egg to the mixture, beating all the time, until it is incorporated smoothly. Fold in the flour and baking powder, followed by the date mixture.
4 Grease a 1.7-litre basin with a little butter, put a circle of baking paper in the bottom, grease that, sprinkle in some caster sugar, then tap out any excess. Half fill with the mixture and cover with foil.
5 Put in a bain-marie (or roasting pan filled with hot water to come halfway up the sides of the basin) and bake for about 50 minutes until well risen and springy to the touch. If you insert a skewer into the centre of the pudding it should come out clean.
6 Turn the pudding out and serve with Toffee Sauce (see page 94) and Custard (see opposite).

Custard All good puddings need custard. Crème pâtissière, or confectioner's custard, is the first recipe I ever made in a professional kitchen at the age of sixteen, and I still have the proportions locked in my head.

You can serve it cold or hot, or use it to line fruit tarts. Mix it with equal quantities of cream and use it for filling choux pastry buns or doughnuts. If you want to make chocolate custard, replace 15 g of the plain flour with 15 g of cocoa. To stop custard from forming a skin on top if you are keeping it in the fridge, sprinkle it with sugar and put a sheet of baking paper over the top while it is still warm.

In that first kitchen, no one thought to do that, so we apprentices used to strip the skins off the tops of the big custard containers all in one piece, put them shiny side down on a board, sprinkle with sugar, then cover them with strawberry jam, roll them up and eat like crêpes. Comfort food and a sense of naughtiness go hand in hand!

> **❛Comfort food and a sense of naughtiness go hand in hand!❜**

Makes about 1 litre

1 litre milk
1 vanilla pod
120 g sugar (preferably vanilla)
8 egg yolks
40 g flour
40 g cornflour

1 Put the milk in a pan with the vanilla pod and bring to the boil.
2 Whisk the sugar with the egg yolks in a large heatproof bowl until the mixture is pale. Incorporate the flour and cornflour a little at a time.
3 Very gradually pour a little boiling milk over the mixture, whisking all the time. When that is fully incorporated, add a little more milk and so on until it's all taken up.
4 Pour the mixture back into the pan and cook it gently over a very low heat, stirring all the time, until the custard is smooth and thick.

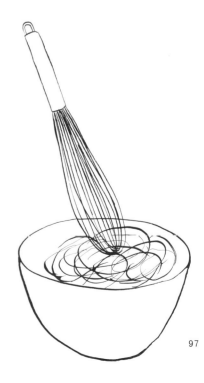

Comfort

Poached Tamarillos with Cheesecake

Serves 8

Whenever I poach fruit in wintertime it reminds me of bright icy days and that exhilarating exhaustion you feel at the end of a hard day's skiing, when some kind person hands you a steaming mug of *gluwein* or *vin chaud*. If big pots of red wine with cinnamon and spices mulling on the stove aren't comforting, I don't know what is.

Cinnamon sticks are lovely objects when you look at them closely: tight tan-coloured suede-like rolls of dried bark from evergreen trees (part of the laurel family) which are sliced off by hand by workers shinning up the trunks in Sri Lanka, the Seychelles and various Caribbean islands. When I can find them, I often use chippings of the outside bark, which is rougher and more dusty-flavoured and adds a bit more texture and warmth to the wine in this recipe.

Then there are the vanilla pods, the best and most luxurious of which come from Madagascar. I hate to see people using a pristine new pod then dropping it in the bin. I keep them in jars of caster sugar, so the sugar takes on a great vanilla flavour for making custard, then my son Marcel will drop one into his milk to flavour it, it will get washed and dried, and put back in the sugar to be used again. Even when you have scraped all the seeds into a custard or sauce, the pods still retain their incredible flavour for a long time.

You can poach firm pears or figs in the same way as the tamarillos and serve them with ice-cream if you don't feel like making cheesecake. After you've taken the fruit out of the poaching liquor it can be bubbled up in the pan over a medium heat, to reduce it down to a thick syrup. I also like the idea of keeping some warm unreduced liquor back to serve in a glass, with a vanilla pod stirrer.

8 tamarillos
500 ml red wine, like a fruity vin de pays
100 g caster sugar
3 vanilla beans
1 cinnamon stick
5 blades of mace

1 Score the pointed end of the tamarillos through in the shape of a cross, as with Brussels sprouts, then put in a large pan with the rest of the ingredients and 500 ml water. Bring to the boil, turn the heat down and bubble gently for 10 minutes.
2 Remove from the heat, cover and leave the fruit to cool in the juices before removing.
3 If you like, bubble up the juices until they are reduced to a syrup. Serve with the Vanilla Cheesecake overleaf.

Vanilla Cheesecake

Makes 1 large cake

1 small packet of good-quality
  digestive biscuits
70 g butter, softened
700 ml whipping cream
120 g caster sugar
700 g cream cheese
1 teaspoon vanilla extract
seeds from 1 vanilla pod

1 Crush the biscuits, mix well with the
butter, then press the crumbs into the
base of a big cake tin.
2 Put the rest of the ingredients into a
mixing bowl and whisk until thick.
3 Spoon the mixture on top of the
biscuit base and smooth the top with a
palette knife.
4 Leave in the fridge to chill for about 2
hours, until completely set.
5 Serve with the poached tamarillos
(see previous page) and, if you like, the
reduced poaching liquor.

Chocolate Brownies

Makes about 16

140 g butter, plus more for greasing
50 g cocoa
2 eggs
225 g caster sugar
drop of vanilla extract
70 g toasted hazelnuts, roughly
  chopped
100 g plain flour

1 Preheat the oven to 180°C/350°F/gas 4.
Grease a 20 cm square cake tin or
baking pan with butter and line with
baking paper.
2 Put the butter in a heavy-based pan
with the cocoa and heat very gently until
the butter melts.
3 In a mixing bowl, beat the eggs and
caster sugar together until the mixture
is pale.
4 Slowly beat in the butter and cocoa
mixture. Add the vanilla extract and stir
in well. Fold in the chopped toasted
nuts and the flour.
5 Pour the mixture into the prepared
baking tin and bake in the preheated
oven for 20–25 minutes until just firm to
the touch.
6 Leave to cool in the tin, then cut into
squares to serve.

Classic

On one weekend that my family won't let me forget I sulked all day over a dozen eggs. I had bought some free-range organic farmhouse beauties, so that on Sunday morning we could have French toast. I just love that soggy eggy bread with stacks of crispy bacon. Just as I was having a shower and thinking about breakfast, there was a big smashing sound from the kitchen. Three-year-old Marcel was swinging backwards and forwards on the fridge and had managed to knock out the box of eggs and drop the lot on the floor. So I made bacon sandwiches and moped around melodramatically.

I can taste the flavour of French toast so vividly just talking about it, and I think we all have moments when we want to eat and cook something that feels familiar, however simple, that has been made by millions of people, time and time again, and will continue to be cooked and enjoyed, because it just works so well.

I guess everyone has their own definition of classic. For some people, the words classic and French are interchangeable. Like most young Australians starting out in cooking, I initially snubbed anything French, then I grew up and realized that, for a chef, that is like trying to study English literature without reading Shakespeare.

Of course the French classic cuisine repertoire is huge, but there are also wonderful classic dishes from China, Russia, America... and as food continues to evolve, cooks will keep coming up with dishes that will stand the test of time and join the list of great recipes from around the world. The *Oxford Reference Dictionary* defines classical as 'of acknowledged excellence', 'simple and harmonious in style', clear and logical in contrast to an 'irrational display of personal emotion'. If you throw ingredients around for fashion rather than flavour, you are never going to create a classic dish. However, Chinese roast duck, a platter of *choucroute* or *crème brûlée* are

> **‹ For some people, the words classic and French are interchangeable ›**

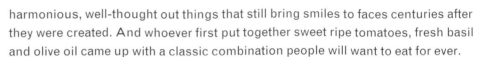

Classic

> **I think a classic is a dish that – done properly – is very difficult to improve upon**

harmonious, well-thought out things that still bring smiles to faces centuries after they were created. And whoever first put together sweet ripe tomatoes, fresh basil and olive oil came up with a classic combination people will want to eat for ever.

I think a classic is a dish that – done properly – is very difficult to improve upon. You can adapt it if you want to, but you will rarely make it better, because the essential combination of flavours and techniques is too good to change. Take a dish like *bouillabaisse*: everyone has their own idea about what fish should go into it, but they all agree that this fish stew has to be boiled quite violently – in a way you wouldn't normally treat fish – to produce the essential amalgamation of olive oil and water.

You can argue about the all the fine details, and people get pretty heated up about all that stuff – whether a true *salade niçoise* should have tuna in it, or anchovies, or both; whether you can make a real *coq au vin* if the wine isn't from Burgundy, whether to use wine, malt or balsamic vinegar in your salad of tomatoes, basil and oil – but that's great. Half the fun of eating and cooking is stirring up controversy. I upset plenty of people by putting anchovies in my Caesar salad dressing, but I don't care because it tastes great, and to me it is entirely in the spirit of the dish!

What isn't so great about the classics is that they have often been done badly over the years. Take *spaghetti alla carbonara*. In its basic form, it is beautiful: boiling-hot spaghetti tossed at the table with pancetta and shaved parmesan and raw eggs that set softly around the slightly firm pasta. Over the years, however, people have added cream and wine, and other cheeses, and made up a sauce in advance, so that what passes for *carbonara* bears little relation to that original charming little dish.

People find it hard to resist playing around with classics, just because they think that they are too simple, that you can't give a dinner party and serve a bowl of pasta with bacon and eggs in it. Why not, if it is great pasta? Relax and stop worrying about trying to impress with complicated dishes. What's wrong with buying the best piece of steak you can afford, making a classic Béarnaise sauce and serving them with a big bowl of well-cooked chips and a great bottle of red wine?

Eggs I think eggs are wonderful things, one of the most versatile ingredients in the world, though I can never quite forget the scene in the movie *Angel Heart* in which the Lucifer character, played by Robert De Niro, declares that the egg is the symbol of the soul and then devours it. American diners are the place for terrific eggs, and brunch dishes like eggs Benedict and eggs Florentine are undoubtedly modern classics. It's also hard to beat great steak and eggs and a Bloody Mary or a soft poached egg breaking into corned beef hash.

If I make Bollito Misto (page 113) for friends on a Saturday night, I'll keep back about 250 g of the cooked salt beef in the fridge to make ✳ **Corned Beef Hash** in the morning. To make enough for 2 people you need to take the piece of cold beef and grate it, then grate about 300 g of boiled potato, mix the two together and season it all really well. Put about a tablespoon of butter in a big frying pan with roughly 1½ tablespoons of olive oil. Get it hot, put in the potato and beef mixture, and flatten it out like a pancake. Cook it fairly gently, until you can see the base turning golden and crispy, then flip it over with a spatula. It doesn't matter if it breaks up, just press it down again into a pancake-shape.

When the underside crisps up, scatter a couple of handfuls of baby spinach over one half of the corned beef hash, then fold the other side over the top, like an omelette. Turn out on a plate, then cut into two and top each half with a poached egg. You can make ✳ **Hash Browns** in the same way, leaving out the corned beef, and serve them with crispy bacon or thick pieces of ham instead.

And if you want to make ✳ **French Toast**, just beat your eggs – preferably tasty free-range organic farmhouse! – then cut some thick slices of good white bread, dip them into the beaten eggs seasoned with lots of salt and black pepper – get them good and sodden – then fry them on both sides in butter in a hot frying pan.

Eggs Benedict

I know people get put off making eggs Benedict simply because they are intimidated by the idea of making hollandaise sauce, but as long as you take it nice and gently – adding the butter a little at a time, just like adding olive oil to eggs for mayonnaise – the result should be fine. If at any time while you are adding the butter you are frightened that the sauce is going to split, beat in a tablespoon of hot water to stabilize it, then carry on.

There is also a cheat's way of making hollandaise, which is to use the vinegar reduction while it is very hot, pour it into a bowl with the rest of the ingredients except the butter, blast it with a hand-held blender, then add the melted butter bit by bit, still whizzing with the blender, until it is all amalgamated smoothly. It won't hold as well as the traditionally beaten sauce, but if you use it straight away, it will be almost as good.

I love hollandaise in this dish with the soft eggs and chunky ham, but I also have a weakness for hollandaise served with salmon, or chips!

8 eggs
dash of white wine vinegar
4 muffins
a little butter
8 thick slices of smoked ham

for the Hollandaise Sauce:
6 tablespoons white wine
6 tablespoons white wine vinegar
20 black peppercorns
2 bay leaves
3 egg yolks
300 g melted butter
pinch of salt
juice of ½ lemon

1 First start by making the hollandaise sauce: put the white wine and white wine vinegar in a saucepan together with the black peppercorns and the bay leaves. Bring the mixture to the boil, then let it bubble rapidly for about 5–8 minutes, until the liquid reduces down to about 3 tablespoons only. Leave this reduction to cool, then remove the black peppercorns and the bay leaves.

Bloody Mary

This is for quite a spicy drink; but you can hot it up even further as you like.

Makes 2 large ones

200 ml vodka
500 ml tomato juice
3 drops of Worcestershire
  sauce
4 drops of Tabasco sauce
½ teaspoon grated fresh
  horseradish
2 shakes of celery salt
juice of ½ lemon
couple of grinds of black
  pepper

Stir all the ingredients together in a jug and pour over ice into highball glasses.

2 Break the egg yolks into a big non-reactive metal bowl, place it over a pan of barely simmering water, and whisk in about a tablespoon of the vinegar reduction (I usually measure it in half an eggshell). Continue to whisk the egg yolks for a few minutes until the mixture turns pale and the whisk begins to leave ribbon-like marks.

3 Remove from the heat and, little by little, whisk in the melted butter, making sure each addition is whisked in completely before adding any more. Keep going until all the butter is incorporated and the sauce is thick and creamy. Have a bowl of hot water handy, so that you can add a tablespoon if you feel that it might be about to scramble. Beat in the salt and lemon juice. Set aside, keeping it warm.

4 Poach the eggs in simmering water with a touch of vinegar added for 2 minutes.

5 While the eggs are cooking, cut the muffins in half and toast them on each side until nice and golden. Top each half with a little butter.

6 Place 2 muffin halves on each plate and top each with a slice of ham. Place a poached egg on the top of each piece. Then pour the hollandaise over the top.

Baked Eggs, Spinach, Ham and Cream
Serves 2

40 g butter
4 good handfuls of baby spinach leaves
salt and freshly ground black pepper
3 tablespoons double cream
4 eggs
2 slices of Bayonne or other cured ham

1 Preheat the oven to 200°C/400°F/gas 6.
2 In a heavy ovenproof frying pan, heat the butter until golden and slightly nutty. Add the spinach and let it wilt.
3 Season, pour in the cream and let it boil up.
4 Crack the eggs on top, then very gently lay the ham over them. Transfer the pan to the oven for about 7 minutes until the eggs are cooked.

The other classic dish made with eggs and spinach is ✳ **Eggs Florentine**, which consists of toasted muffins, topped with spinach cooked in a little butter and black pepper, and then poached eggs, all smothered in a béchamel sauce enriched with cream and egg yolks to give it a sheen when it is finished off under the grill.

The basic ✳ **Béchamel Sauce** is made with 1 part butter and 1 part flour to 10 parts milk. For 4 people you need to melt around 40 g butter in a pan, then mix with 40 g flour and cook very gently, stirring, for about a minute. Take the pan off the heat and gradually whisk in 400 ml milk, a very small amount at first, until it all goes in smoothly. Put the pan back on the heat and cook very gently, until you have a thick white sauce. Take the pan off the heat again and gently fold in 5 tablespoons double cream. Don't beat or you will thicken the cream too much. Allow to cool slightly, then mix in one egg yolk.

Assemble your muffins, spinach and eggs and place in a heatproof dish, pour the sauce over and put under a preheated grill until the sauce turns golden and glazed.

Salade Niçoise

Ask any group of cooks what they like to put into their *salade niçoise* and before you know it, you are caught up in a hotbed of controversy. Most people agree that a *salade niçoise* should contain black olives, lettuce, tomatoes and anchovies – but what else? Elizabeth David in *A Book of Mediterranean Food* talks evocatively of *pan bagnia*: crusty bread, filled with black olives, strips of sweet pepper, tomatoes, young raw broad beans, and a dressing of olive oil and vinegar, eaten with a bottle of wine over a game of *boules*. This, she reckons, was the forerunner of the *salade niçoise*; other people think it was possibly the other way round.

I think the traditional salad would definitely have been made with anchovies, but should there be tuna, and if so should we call the dish 'tuna niçoise'? Perhaps that is the safest idea. However, should the tuna be fresh or tinned? I can understand why tinned tuna is considered more authentic than fresh, because at one time the cooked fish was probably preserved in oil, so that the salad could be made all year round. My theory is that it would have been made with fresh or preserved tuna, according to season. Since I hate canned tuna, though, I always cook fresh tuna in olive oil.

What about the other ingredients: should you use broad beans, or the long haricots verts? Can you add cooked potatoes, or artichoke hearts, or *anything* cooked? Some people say the whole point of the salad is that the vegetables in it should all be raw and crunchy, and include raw peppers, onions, fennel or celery. Again, I feel that people in the past would have traditionally used whatever fresh produce was available at the time of year, be it new cooked potatoes or raw young broad beans.

Finally there is the question of eggs. Some people make artistic little salads with quails' eggs, which I really don't agree with, mainly because I have difficulty thinking of quails' eggs as real at all. Robert De Niro would never have been able to crunch into a quail's egg with the same effect!

'Ask any group of cooks what they like to put into their *salade niçoise* and before you know it, you are caught up in a hotbed of controversy'

Tuna Salade Niçoise

A chef I worked with in Australia used to put scrubbed rocks around the tuna when he cooked it in oil, to displace the liquid and raise the level, thus avoiding using gallons of oil. You could use anything you like, such as upturned ramekin dishes, to fill up the spaces around the fish.

The best anchovies to use are fresh ones; usually they are kept in tubs of brine. If you can't find them, the beautiful Spanish ones packed in salt are the next best thing, though they can be fiddly to fillet. Jars of anchovies in oil are pretty good too. Again the Spanish ones are great and they are often already filleted, but avoid the cheaper anchovies that come in tins, or stuffed with capers, because they don't have the depth of flavour you need.

Some people would say that the dressing for a *salade niçoise* shouldn't be creamy, but I like it that way. If you are worried about the raw egg or prefer a more oily dressing, however, just leave the egg out.

Classic

'Some people make artistic little salads with quails' eggs, which I really don't agree with, mainly because I have difficulty thinking of quails' eggs as real at all'

Tuna Salade Niçoise

1 kg fresh tuna, trimmed
1 carrot, halved lengthwise
1 celery stalk
white of 1 small leek, slit lengthwise
few sprigs of thyme and flat parsley
1 chilli, split in half and deseeded
4 garlic cloves
2 bay leaves
salt and freshly ground black pepper
about 1 litre olive oil
4 eggs
200 g green beans
150 g pitted black olives
12 small vine tomatoes, halved
handful of basil leaves
16 boiled small new potatoes, halved
1 small red onion, sliced
about 20 anchovy fillets (see page 105)

for the dressing:
3 tablespoons red wine vinegar
1 teaspoon Dijon mustard
1 egg yolk (optional, see page 105)
250 ml olive oil

1 Put the tuna in a big pot with the
carrot, celery, leek, thyme and some
parsley stalks tied in a bundle. Add the
chilli, garlic, bay leaves and seasoning.
Cover with olive oil and place over a
slow heat until big bubbles break the
surface. Take off the heat immediately
and let the tuna cool in the liquid.
2 To make the dressing: process the
vinegar, mustard and egg yolk, if using,
until the mixture turns white. Season and,
with the machine still running, very slowly
add the oil until it is all incorporated.
3 Boil the eggs for 3–4 minutes, cool
under cold running water and then
shell. Blanch the beans briefly in boiling
water, then plunge them into cold water.
4 When the tuna is cool, remove it from
the oil. Strain that and, if you like, keep a
little back to stir into the dressing. (Keep
the rest in the fridge for use next time you
cook tuna – but first boil it and remove
any impurities that come to the surface.
5 Break the tuna into shards and mound
up with the remaining ingredients. Drizzle
with dressing and scatter with parsley.

Caesar Salad with Anchovies In New York I recently ate a great Caesar salad which consisted of a whole Cos lettuce halved lengthwise and served just as it was with the dressing drizzled over. If you've got a great lettuce, why not, because that's what this dish is about, the contrast of really fresh, crunchy, moist lettuce and a thick, creamy, garlicky dressing. In another New York restaurant I saw a Caesar salad served with a one-eyed Susie, an egg fried inside a scooped-out round of bread, like an oversized crouton. When cut into, the yolk oozed out into the dressed leaves: clever stuff, but for me it doesn't quite capture the essence of a Caesar salad.

> **ʻThat is what this dish is about, the contrast of really fresh crunchy moist lettuce and a really thick creamy, garlicky dressingʼ**

4 little gem lettuces
about 20 anchovy fillets
some parmesan shavings, to serve

for the dressing:
1 whole egg, plus 1 extra egg yolk
2 teaspoons white wine vinegar
2 teaspoons Dijon mustard
1 garlic clove, crushed
200 ml vegetable oil, plus more for frying
150 g grated parmesan cheese
2 anchovy fillets, chopped

for the croutons:
3 thick slices of day-old white bread
100 g pancetta, cut into pieces
1 garlic clove, finely chopped
salt
25 g grated parmesan cheese

1 To make the dressing: whisk the egg, egg yolk, white wine vinegar, Dijon mustard and crushed garlic until the mixture starts to thicken and turn white. Slowly add the vegetable oil and whisk in. You might need a little hot water to thin the dressing slightly. Finally whisk in the grated parmesan and the chopped anchovies.

2 To make the croutons: cut the crusts off the day-old white bread, then cut it into in good-sized pieces. Heat about a centimetre of the vegetable oil in a frying pan or a wok (which is what I like to use), then put in the pieces of pancetta and fry them until they are nice and crispy. Put in the pieces of bread and keep moving them around all the time until they are crispy and

golden, then scatter some of the chopped garlic over them.

3 Using a slotted spoon, transfer the fried croutons and the pancetta to a bowl (you can keep the oil in the fridge for use another time), toss them around to cool a little, then add some salt and the grated parmesan while the croutons are still just warm, so that the cheese sticks to the outside, making them lovely and crunchy while they are still soft and pillowy inside.

4 Toss the lettuce leaves well in the dressing and pile them into a large bowl or 4 small ones. Sprinkle with the croutons and pancetta, and the whole anchovy fillets, then scatter over some more parmesan in the form of shavings (use a swivel peeler on a block of the cheese to make them).

Stracciatella This is a Roman dish, one of the simplest soups in the world, but there is something about the soft strands of egg in the very light broth that is very clean and fresh. It is not unlike Chinese egg-flower soups, in which the chicken stock is flavoured with garlic, ginger and spring onion, and just before serving beaten egg is trailed through it over the prongs of a fork so that it sets in strands. This recipe gives you a basic chicken stock which you can use for other things. If you want a darker stock for a different dish, roast the bones lightly in the oven before you put them into the pot.

4 large eggs
handful of grated parmesan cheese
salt and freshly ground black pepper

for the chicken stock:
1 kg chicken pieces, such as wings
   and thighs
handful of chopped leeks
handful of chopped carrot
handful of chopped celery
few sprigs of herbs, such as parsley,
   thyme and rosemary
a few black peppercorns
2 bay leaves
4 slices of crusty bread, to serve
   (optional)

1 At least 4 hours ahead, make the stock: put the chicken pieces in a large pot with the rest of the stock ingredients and cover with about 4 litres of cold water. It must be cold so that the juices are brought out slowly and to help any impurities congeal and rise to the top. They can then be skimmed off to stop the stock from tasting bitter. Bring to the boil and then immediately reduce the heat to a simmer and cook at this gentle level of bubbling for about 3 hours, regularly skimming the surface.

2 Sieve into a bowl and leave to cool. Keep in the fridge until ready to make your soup, then skim off any surface fat.

3 Pour the clear stock carefully into a pan, discarding any dark sediment at the bottom of the bowl. Bring the stock to the boil. While it heats through, whisk the eggs with the parmesan and season.

4 Turn the stock down to a very gentle simmer, pour the egg mix into it and remove from the heat. Stir with a fork.

5 Pour into bowls, preferably over a slice of good crusty bread, which will turn deliciously soggy and puffy.

Classic

Spaghetti alla Carbonara

Serve this with a good loaf of bread and a simple salad of ripe tomatoes and basil leaves dressed with a little olive oil and vinegar.

Serves 4–6

sea salt
a little olive oil
500 g dried durum wheat spaghetti
4 large egg yolks
freshly ground black pepper
200 g thick slices of pancetta or
 smoked bacon
good handful of freshly grated
 parmesan

1 Bring 5 litres of water to the boil in a big pan with a pinch of salt and a dash of olive oil. Put in the spaghetti, coiling it around the pan and pushing it under the water. Stir with a fork to separate the strands. Cook for about 7 minutes at a good rolling boil, or according to the packet instructions, until *al dente*, i.e. cooked but still with a little bite to it.

2 While the spaghetti is cooking, beat the egg yolks and season with the pepper. Get a serving bowl hot and cut the pancetta or bacon into strips.

3 When the pasta is almost done, heat some more olive oil in another large pan (big enough to take the cooked spaghetti) and fry the pancetta or bacon until it is well coloured and beginning to crisp up.

4 Drain the spaghetti and add to the pan of pancetta or bacon, tossing everything well so that the pasta takes up all the oil. Season with some more black pepper.

5 Take the pan off the heat and add the beaten egg yolk and parmesan, and continue to toss until the eggs begin to turn creamy and just start to set.

6 Serve immediately.

' Everyone has their own idea of what an authentic *bouillabaisse* should be '

Bouillabaisse This is another controversial dish, and not because of the way you cook it (the word comes from a mixture of *bouiller*, which means 'to boil', and *abaisser*, 'to reduce'). It's the fish you put into it that gets the arguments going. Everyone has their own idea of what an authentic *bouillabaisse* should be. In Marseilles there is even a charter drawn up by restaurateurs agreeing to preserve what they consider to be the 'real' recipe.

Originally *bouillabaisse* was just a big fish stew cooked by fishermen over an open fire on the beach at the end of the day, and made with whatever fish and shellfish weren't good enough to send to market. I think it needs that feel of the fresh catch, straight from the sea, and that's when I prefer to eat or cook it – on holiday by the Mediterranean, when there will be all sorts of fish available and you can make a party of cooking the likes of bream, monkfish, mullet, sea bass and John Dory in a great big tureen. However, you can use the recipe loosely and add whatever fresh fish you prefer.

I serve it with some *rouille* (garlic mayonnaise) spread over large croutons that have first been rubbed with garlic. If you're concerned about raw eggs, it might be better to buy some good ready-made mayonnaise and spice it up with finely chopped garlic and chillies.

Serves 8

about 175 ml olive oil
2 small whole red mullet
1 small whole John Dory
2 gurnard steaks, each about 125 g
24 medium mussels
24 large clams
16 langoustines
24 whole plum tomatoes
1 whole fennel bulb, sliced
4 garlic cloves, finely chopped
about 2 litres fish stock

for the rouille:
pinch of saffron strands
2 garlic cloves, chopped
1 chilli, deseeded and chopped
2 egg yolks
70 g cooked potatoes
300 ml olive oil
salt and freshly ground black pepper

for the croutons:
1 baguette, sliced
olive oil for frying
1 fat garlic clove, halved

1 First make the *rouille*: get a pan hot on the hob, then take it to one side, add the saffron and stir around the pan until it colours and releases its aroma. Put the saffron in a food processor with the garlic, chilli and egg yolks, and blitz to a paste. Add the potatoes and process a little more until all the ingredients are combined. With the motor still running, add the oil a little at a time until you have a thick mayonnaise-like sauce. Adjust the seasoning.

2 Heat the olive oil in a pan big enough to take all the fish and shellfish, and gently fry the plum tomatoes and fennel until coloured on the outside and soft in the middle. Add the garlic for the last few minutes.

3 Add half the fish stock and bring to the boil, then turn down the heat and add the whole fish and pieces. Boil rapidly for about 10 minutes.

4 Meanwhile, clean and scrub the mussels and clams in plenty of running water, discarding any that won't close when tapped, and set aside.

5 Add the mussels, clams and langoustines to the stock and carry on boiling for 4–5 minutes until the mussels and clams have opened. Discard any that don't. Take out the langoustines, split them down the centre, then put them back. By now the fish should be cooked.

6 While the seafood is finishing, make the croutons: fry the baguette slices in hot oil until golden on both sides. Rub them with the halved garlic.

7 Season the bouillabaisse if necessary, transfer to a big warmed bowl and serve the croutons and the *rouille* on the side.

Roast Whole Turbot

A much simpler – but I think very classic – thing to do if you want to serve fish is to roast a whole turbot of about 1–1½ kg. Slash the skin in criss-crosses, season and drizzle with a little olive oil. Preheat the oven to 240°C/475°F/gas 9, then put the fish into a big ovenproof dish, pour about a tablespoon of white wine and a teaspoon of water over the top, add a few sprigs of lemon thyme and cook for 12–15 minutes, basting regularly. The skin should blister, but the flesh inside will stay moist.

While the fish is in the oven, cook some shallots in hot oil in a pan until golden and just soft, add a handful of black olives, stir for a few minutes and serve around the fish, with some wedges of lemon. Take off the top fillet first, then lift out the bone, tail end first, to get at the bottom fillet, rather than turning the fish over as, according to an old superstition, you will tip the boat over and the fishermen will fall out!

Bollito Misto This is an Italian party feast, not worth doing in full unless you have a dozen people to help you eat it. Then it makes a really simple but quite decadent meal. It is a great ice-breaker because there is a lot of passing around of food and sharing. As so often in cooking superstition, the magic number for the ultimate *bollito misto* is seven: seven different meats, which means you need an enormous pot – one of those big *Macbeth* cauldrons would do fine. On the other hand, for a smaller occasion you can make a scaled-down version, with perhaps a chicken, a veal shank and a cotechino sausage.

I know that for some people the idea of boiling things like chicken or beef has connotations of grey tasteless meat, and it is true that in the old days at the Italian court and in wealthy households the gentry got the consommé – the gorgeously flavoursome liquid full of goodness in which the meat was cooked – and the meat itself, with all the flavour sucked out of it during an incredibly long cooking time, was given to the peasants.

In Eastern Europe, *borscht* is made following the same principles, but with grated beetroot squeezed into the broth at the end. The meat – traditionally cheaper cuts such as veal shins and pork knuckles – is quite tasteless by the end of the long cooking time and is discarded, leaving all its nourishment in the broth. The idea of a modern *bollito misto* is to keep the meat boiling gently for not too long, without stirring things around, so that all the meats and the vegetables stay whole and you hit the balance of great stock and lovely tender meat retaining all its flavour.

The classic way to serve *bollito misto* is with bowls of Salsa Verde (see page 84) and mustard fruits, which are candied fruits preserved in a sweet translucent syrup spiced up with mustard seeds. You can buy jars of mustard fruits (the best are mostarda di Cremona) from good Italian delis.

Serves 12–16

4 carrots
4 onions
4 celery stalks
1 pig's trotter
3 sprigs of sage
1 teaspoon black peppercorns
1 kg veal shank, bone in
1 kg salt beef
1 large boiling chicken
sea salt
1 cotechino (Italian pork salame) or
    similar sausage
1 zampone (Italian sausage in an outer
    casing of pig's trotter)
1 kg cooked pickled ox tongue

to serve:
bowl of Salsa Verde (see page 84)
bowl of mustard fruits (see above)

1 Put the whole vegetables in the largest pot you can find, followed by the pig's trotter. Cover with plenty of cold water, then add the sage and the peppercorns. Bring to the boil, to 'wash' the trotter, then discard the water.
2 Put in the veal shank and salt beef and start again with fresh cold water to cover. Cook at a slow simmer for about 2 hours, skimming off any impurities from the surface at regular intervals. (The idea of this dish is to end up with really clear, pure stock.)

3 Put in the chicken and add more cold water to cover. Bring up to the boil again, skim the surface as before, then turn the heat back down to a slow simmer. Cook for another 1½ hours or so, until all the meat is cooked. Add salt if necessary.

4 Put in the cotechino, zampone and the ox tongue. Top up with cold water again, bring to the boil and skim the surface, then turn the heat down to produce a slow simmer and cook for another 30 minutes or so, until the sausage, zampone and ox tongue are heated right through and the broth is lovely and rich and clear.

5 Remove each piece of meat from the pot and put them on plates in the middle of the table. Take out the vegetables and cut into small pieces. Cut all the meats up into chunky pieces and let people help themselves to them, the vegetable pieces, mustard fruits and salsa verde.

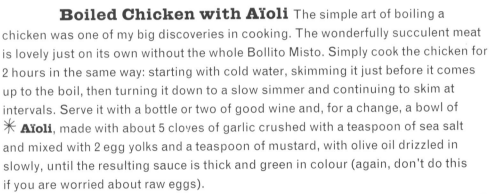

Boiled Chicken with Aïoli The simple art of boiling a chicken was one of my big discoveries in cooking. The wonderfully succulent meat is lovely just on its own without the whole Bollito Misto. Simply cook the chicken for 2 hours in the same way: starting with cold water, skimming it just before it comes up to the boil, then turning it down to a slow simmer and continuing to skim at intervals. Serve it with a bottle or two of good wine and, for a change, a bowl of
✳ **Aïoli**, made with about 5 cloves of garlic crushed with a teaspoon of sea salt and mixed with 2 egg yolks and a teaspoon of mustard, with olive oil drizzled in slowly, until the resulting sauce is thick and green in colour (again, don't do this if you are worried about raw eggs).

I love it when people talk about serving a 'chicken dinner', it sounds so good, and with a chicken boiled in this way you really could do a whole meal, starting with the clear stock served as a consommé, perhaps with dumplings and the vegetables from the pot chopped up. Alternatively, you could mix beaten egg and parmesan into it to make a Stracciatella (see page 109), before serving the chicken and aïoli.

The other chicken classic, of course, is ✳ **Coq au Vin**. Elizabeth David cooked her chicken whole, then caramelized her onions in butter and sugar and put them in at the end. Other people prefer to joint their fowl and add the mushrooms for the last few minutes. Some people reckon you should use a tough boiling fowl, others a plumper bird. What do I think? I reckon it is important to use a chicken with quite a bit of fat in it, not a scrawny thing, and don't kill the texture by overcooking.

Cut the chicken into pieces, then fry them in plenty of butter with a dozen or so small peeled onions and a piece of pancetta or smoked belly bacon, chopped into cubes, or some ready-prepared smoked lardons. When everything colours, pop in a couple of whole garlic cloves, then pour in a whole bottle of good red wine, something with a bit of body. I always think it is a lovely extravagant sound – a whole bottle of wine glugging into a cooking pot.

Bring the whole thing to the boil on the hob, then cover with a tight-fitting lid and put in the oven preheated to 200°C/400°F/gas 6 for a good 1–1 ½ hours. When it is cooked through, fry another dozen small peeled onions in butter until just soft, add a couple of handfuls of mushrooms, season well and toss until they are just golden. Tip them into the pot with loads of chopped parsley and serve.

Sometimes I start off the casserole in the same way, but use white wine and add some thyme. At the end I just add mushrooms, cooked briefly in butter, and a little red wine, which adds a bit of colour. There's no reason why you couldn't make either version with guinea fowl, or brown some rabbit pieces with pancetta or smoked bacon and some onions, and put them into the casserole with white wine, thyme, some green olives and half a lemon. Cook for about 2 hours, or a bit longer if using a wild rabbit.

> **'I reckon it is important to use a chicken with quite a bit of fat in it, not a scrawny thing'**

Chinese Roast Duck with Pancakes

I am a great believer in intensifying flavour in any way you can, so before roasting Chinese ducks I always put some sugar, spices and chopped spring onions inside, which adds enormously to the taste and also helps to tenderize the meat.

The reason for buying Chinese ducks, or Peking ducks as they are often called in supermarkets, is that they are bred to have less fat, so the skin crisps up much better.

I usually roast two ducks at a time and then freeze one. You then just have to defrost it and put it in the oven to heat it all the way through.

Serves 6–8 with other dishes

1 large Chinese duck
2 tablespoons sugar
2 tablespoons sea salt
a few star anise seeds
about 6 cm root ginger, peeled and sliced
1 spring onion, roughly chopped
2 tablespoons maltose
2½ tablespoons red wine vinegar

to serve:
bunch of spring onions, shredded
  lengthwise
1 cucumber, deseeded and cut into
  thin strips
hoisin sauce
Chinese pancakes (about 6 per person)

The day before:

1 Wash the duck inside and out with cold water, drain and pat dry. Bring a kettle of water to the boil.

2 Mix together the sugar, sea salt, star anise, ginger and spring onions and use to fill the cavity, then secure it with a wooden skewer, soaked first in water so that it doesn't splinter.

3 In a small pan, mix the maltose with 2 tablespoons of the vinegar and a table-spoon of boiling water. Bring to the boil.

4 Add the remaining vinegar to a jugful of the boiling water and pour over the duck. The boiling water opens up the pores, while the vinegar helps to strip some of the waxiness from the skin, so it will be more receptive to the maltose.

5 Spoon the boiling maltose mixture over the duck, baste another four times, then hang up to dry overnight.

Next day:

6 Preheat the oven to 220°C/425°F/gas 7. Put a little water in the bottom of a roasting tin and place the duck on a rack over the top. Roast for 1–1½ hours (convection ovens are particularly effective for roasting duck). The duck must be well done – there is no such thing as a rare Chinese roast duck!

7 Using two forks, shred the duck skin and meat and pile on a big warm plate; arrange the spring onions and cucumber on another. Serve the hoisin sauce in a bowl.

8 Meanwhile, steam the pancakes very briefly until warmed through.

9 To make up the pancakes, spread a little hoisin on each one, top with some shredded duck, spring onions and cucumber and roll up like a cigar. Fold over one end and hold on to this as you munch, to stop the filling falling out.

Steak Many people choose steak by looking for something that is uniformly red and not at all fatty, whereas a good steak needs some marbling – tiny veins of fat that melt into the meat and keep it moist when it is cooking. I prefer not to buy steak surrounded by yellow fat, as that usually means it comes from a herd that has been fed on grain, rather than grass. Grass-fed herds, which will have been allowed to roam free, produce meat with a milky-white fat that has the lovely earthy flavour that I prefer.

Fillet is usually thought of as the best cut, and because you get only two very small fillets from each beast, the laws of supply and demand dictate that it is very expensive. Sirloin is usually seen as next best, with rump a poor second cousin. Ever game for a bit of controversy, I disagree. I really love a thick piece of rump cut from a piece of beef that has been hung on the bone to mature for twenty-one days. Fry it very quickly in a really hot pan to seal in the juices, then finish it off in the oven for about 4–6 minutes, until it is medium-rare – fantastic stuff! A really classy piece of rump has all the right ratios of fat, muscle structure, fibre and flavour.

If you are a fan of 'blue' steak, I find it is hard to get it right with the thicker cuts, because to dissolve that fat from the marbling to moisten the meat, you need heat. The only way I think you can do blue steak satisfactorily is with a thin minute steak, flash-fried, so it colours on the outside, but is blue on the inside. That can be quite delicious.

If I buy sirloin, I like a piece with the tail on it, which you can season with lots of salt

❛A really classy piece of rump has all the right ratios of fat, muscle structure, fibre and flavour❜

and pepper, so that nice bit of fat on the end goes beautifully crusty, with a kind of spiciness that doesn't damage the flavour of the meat, but gives you a wonderful zing in the mouth. Whatever cut you are using, remember to remove the steak from the fridge well ahead of time to give it a chance to get to room temperature before cooking – this is especially important if you like your steak rare.

The two classic steak dishes that will never go out of fashion are steak with Béarnaise sauce (similar to Hollandaise, but made with tarragon) and pepper steak – both served with a bowl of crisp, freshly cooked chips and lots of roast garlic and rosemary.

As a change from chips I sometimes make ✳**Deep-fried Salsify**. I scrub and peel about 500 g, then put it in a bowl of water (with a squeeze of lemon juice to keep its colour) until it is needed. Then I cut it at an angle into chips and put these in a pan of cold water, bring this to the boil, cook for about 5 minutes and drain. When cool, I dip them in beaten egg and then breadcrumbs, and deep-fry them.

Steak Béarnaise

4 rump steaks, each about 300 g
a little butter (optional)
a little olive oil
bunch of watercress, to serve

for the Béarnaise Sauce:
100 ml white wine vinegar
1 shallot, chopped
a few tarragon stalks
3 egg yolks
250 g warm melted butter
salt and freshly ground black pepper

1 Preheat a griddle or the oven to 200°C/400°F/gas 6.

2 Make the Béarnaise Sauce: put the vinegar, shallot and tarragon in a pan and bring to the boil, then cook until reduced by about three-quarters. Let cool and pour into a large stainless-steel bowl .

3 Place the bowl over a pan of just-simmering water, add the egg yolks and whisk until you can see the whisk leaving a trail in the sauce.

4 Remove the bowl from the heat and put it on a folded cloth (to keep the heat in) on a work surface, then start to add the melted butter, little by little, whisking all the time until all the butter is used, or your arm has fallen off!

5 Unless using a griddle plate, heat a little butter in a heavy frying pan.

6 Season the steaks and rub well with olive oil.

7 If using the griddle plate, cook for 3 minutes on a very high heat, turn and cook for a further 3 minutes on the other side, to produce medium-rare steaks. Increase or decrease these times by a minute if you prefer your steaks well done or rare respectively.

8 Alternatively, seal the steaks quickly on both sides in the frying pan and then transfer them to the oven for about 4–6 minutes, depending on how rare you like your meat.

9 Allow the cooked steaks to rest briefly in a warm place, then serve with a little watercress and some of the Béarnaise sauce on the side.

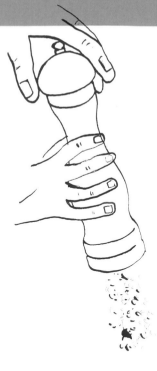

Pepper Steak

This is one steak dish that is best done with fillet, as you need that really good thickness to give a big volume of meat to the pepper, otherwise the result will be uncomfortably hot. I like this steak served with just the buttery, peppery juices, but some people add a touch of cream at the end.

50 g black peppercorns
4 fillet steaks, each about 250 g
75 g butter
4 tablespoons brandy
1 tablespoon double cream
   (optional)

1 Crush the peppercorns using a food processor or mortar and pestle, then sieve to remove all the dust which will otherwise catch in your throat. Press the remainder into either side of the steaks.

2 Heat 50 g of the butter in a heavy frying pan over a medium heat and put in the steaks. Leave them completely alone until you can see they are forming a golden crust underneath, then turn them over and continue to cook until medium-rare, roughly 3 minutes on each side, or to your taste.

3 Remove the steaks from the pan and let them rest in a warm place, then increase the heat under the pan to high. Add 2 tablespoons of water and the brandy, and flame it carefully to burn off the alcohol.

4 Whisk in the rest of the butter, scraping up the caramelized stuff on the bottom of the pan to incorporate all the tasty scraps of meat into the sauce. If using cream, add to the sauce at this point. Either way, bring the sauce briefly to the boil.

5 Pour the sauce over the cooked steaks to serve.

The Australian classic is ✳ **Carpet Bag Steak**, which is just steak, slit through its thickness to make a pouch, stuffed with fresh oysters, then wrapped in strips of streaky bacon or pancetta before being fried in butter in the same way as Pepper Steak. It is important not to drain the oysters of too much of their water (you need to reserve this for later) before stuffing as the saltiness of the water tenderizes and flavours the meat and keeps the oysters lovely and moist. When the steak is cooked to your liking, take it out of the pan, remove the pan from the heat and add the drained oyster juice, then scrape up the bits from the bottom of the pan and pour the resulting liquid over the steak.

   When there are good ceps around I like to serve a plain steak accompanied by ✳ **Cèpes Bordelaise**. When you work in London restaurants, during the mushroom season suppliers regularly turn up with baskets of wild mushrooms. I remember one woman who brought me the most beautiful ceps that were green on their undersides and really thick. I hadn't had a mushroom with that fantastic texture since the puffballs we used to get in Australia. (In August in Britain you could also see puffballs if you caught the London to Cambridge train and looked out into the countryside about 10 minutes before you arrived – great big blobs, dotted all over the fields. Whenever I spotted them I would get a desperate urge to jump off the train and go mushroom-picking.)

You want ceps the caps of which are big enough to fit in the palm of your hand, with stalks that start off quite thin then become bulbous at the bottom. Wipe them clean, then scrape the base where the root used to be. Don't put them under running water, or they will soak it up like sponges. Slice them really thickly, into about 5 pieces. Heat a little olive oil in a pan, season the mushrooms, then cook them like pieces of meat: brown them on one side, then turn them over, take them out of the pan and set aside. Drain off most of the oil, add 2 diced shallots, and cook until they are just translucent, then add 2 chopped garlic cloves, a glassful of red wine, and bubble up to reduce the liquid by about half, scraping up all the bits from the bottom of the pan. Put back the mushrooms, season, and add a squeeze of lemon juice, then serve with your steak.

I keep a great big jar of dried ceps at home, and I often put some into a pepper grinder, and use them as a condiment, freshly ground over a steak or a casserole. They are quite salty, so be careful not to add too much salt as well. Alternatively, I add some to a fresh wild mushroom risotto at the beginning of cooking, to intensify the flavour.

❛I keep a great big jar of dried ceps at home, and I often put some into a pepper grinder, and use them as a condiment❜

121

Classic

Wild Mushroom Risotto If you have the chance to get your hands on some truffles, you can be really indulgent and shave some over the top of this risotto. If you have them a few days in advance, put them inside the bag of rice, which will then pick up their scent and flavour before you start cooking. You could also put some eggs inside the bag, so the truffles can scent them too and you can have truffled scrambled eggs later. Putting some dried ceps into your bag of rice for a while before using it works in a similar, if less opulent, way. The best Arborio rice is highly polished, but has a chalky stripe down each grain, showing it contains a lot of starch, which is what you need for a good risotto.

50 g butter, plus a little more for
   finishing
2 good tablespoons olive oil, plus a little
   extra for frying
4 long shallots, diced
handful of dried ceps
4 garlic cloves, crushed
350 g Arborio rice
1 litre simmering chicken stock
salt and freshly ground black pepper
about 500 g wild mushrooms (such as
   chanterelles, pied de mouton, pied
   bleu and ceps)
handful of chopped parsley
100 g grated parmesan cheese

1 Heat the 50 g of butter and the 2
tablespoons of olive oil in a big heavy-
bottomed pan. Add half the shallots
and cook until just translucent, then
add the dried ceps and 2 of the crushed
garlic cloves, and cook for another 3–4
minutes.
2 Add the rice and stir around for a
couple of minutes to coat and stop it
from sticking.
3 Have your pot of simmering chicken
stock at the ready. It is important that the
stock and rice are of a similar
temperature, so that the heat doesn't
fall when you add the stock. If it does,
the rice may not rehydrate properly,
which will result in the grains being
cooked on the outside but remaining
quite hard on the inside. Add a couple
of ladlefuls of stock and stir around with
a spatula until all the liquid is taken up
and the rice is scraped from the bottom
of the pan. Keep adding stock, stirring
and scraping all the time, to avoid
sticking. After about 15–20 minutes the
rice will be tender but still firm to the bite
and the risotto will be creamy and moist.

4 In the meantime, heat a little olive oil in
another pan and quickly cook the rest of
the shallots and the remaining garlic until
just softened. Season and set aside in a
large bowl.
5 In a clean pan, heat some more olive oil
and cook each variety of mushroom
separately, letting them sear on one side,
then turning them over, and taking them
out when they just colour. Put them all in
the bowl with the reserved shallots and
garlic, season really well and stir in the
chopped parsley.
6 When the risotto is ready, add the
parmesan and butter, then whisk these
like mad into the risotto, so that you get
that wonderful creamy, soft, voluminous
feel. Add your mushroom mixture, adjust
the seasoning,stir around well and serve.

Choucroute Garni The great thing about *choucroute* (basically salted fermented cabbage, seasoned up with aromatics like juniper berries and peppercorns) is that, like Bollito Misto (pages 113–4), you can have the whole *grand garni* of confit duck, pork, sausages, *petit sel* and so on, when you want to have a feast, or just some *choucroute* with sausages on the side.

This is a mid-way version, with a smoked pork hock as well as a few varieties of sausage. However much meat you go for, though, you must have a big bowlful of boiled potatoes and tubfuls of mustard to pass round.

I wouldn't recommend fermenting the cabbage yourself, unless you really want buckets of the stuff hanging around for three weeks or so. Anyway, you can easily buy it already done for you. If you can find it being sold loose, that is often the best. I remember seeing great warehouses filled with buckets of various cabbage mixtures in the market at Rungis outside Paris. Alternatively, buy it in jars from the supermarket.

When I found my original recipe for *choucroute*, I was amazed to see in the ingredients list 'oignon clouté' – now there's a classic little ingredient. When I was at chef school, we were subjected to a band of Swiss lecturers, a bigoted bunch of little men with funny big hats and show-off jackets with their names and accolades emblazoned in multicoloured cottons. I can hear them now in their heavy accents: 'You must make one *oignon clouté* to go with this cabbage. What is an *oignon clouté* Torode?'

'Dunno.'

'Why don't you know. Are you stupid?'

Well, an *oignon clouté* is just an onion studded with three cloves, with the very centre taken out and a bay leaf pushed down the middle; you put it into your pot of *choucroute*.

1 onion
3 cloves
1 bay leaf
50 g goose fat
2 sprigs of thyme
4 juniper berries
1 kg choucroute
1 smoked pork hock
1 carrot, split in half lengthwise
1 good-quality frankfurter
2 pieces of cooked smoked Toulouse
 sausage
2 pieces of cooked Morteaux
 sausage

to serve:
boiled potatoes
Dijon mustard

1 Preheat the oven to 190°C/375°F/gas 5.
2 Stud the onion with cloves. Remove the centre and stuff with the rolled up bay leaf.
3 Heat the fat in a casserole or pan that will transfer to the oven. Add the onion, thyme and juniper berries and cook gently for 2 minutes. Tip in the choucroute, pork hock and carrot and mix everything together. Cover tightly and cook in the oven for 2–3 hours. Check occasionally and, if it looks too dry, add a little water.
4 Put the sausages on top of the casserole and return to the oven for 35 minutes, or until they are piping hot.
5 To serve, pile the choucroute on a big warmed platter, cut the pork into chunks and arrange on top with the sausages. Serve with boiled potatoes and mustard.

Desserts When I think of all the classic desserts that I like, many of them, such as crème brûlée or lemon curd with crostoli biscuits, have that lovely contrast of pillowy softness and delicious crunch... again timeless combinations that never fail to please.

Lemon Curd

This English classic used to crop up everywhere in desserts, tarts and pies.

Makes about 400 g

2 eggs, beaten
200 g caster sugar
juice of 3 lemons and grated zest of 1
100 g unsalted butter

1 Put the eggs and half the sugar in a bowl with 2 tablespoons of the lemon juice and the zest. Place the bowl over a pan of barely simmering water and beat in the butter very slowly until smooth.
2 Gradually beat in the rest of the lemon juice, tasting as you go to get the right degree of sharpness. Allow to cool.
3 Spoon into pots to serve and eat while freshly made..

A really clever dessert is ✳ **Lemon Curd Parfait**. First make up a classic parfait mixture. If you are worried about lightly cooked eggs, make it in the traditional way by cooking 80 g caster sugar with a little water until they form a syrup, then whisking this little by little into 4 egg yolks plus 1 whole egg in a stainless-steel bowl set over a pan of barely simmering water. Keep beating until the mixture is thick and white, adding a few drops of vanilla extract, if you like. Then lightly whip 400 ml of double cream and fold this in. Spoon a layer of mixture into a loaf tin and freeze for about 20 minutes until it starts to firm up, then pipe three stripes of lemon curd down the length, put back in the freezer to firm up some more, spoon in some more parfait mixture, freeze again, and so on, adding more layers of lemon curd and parfait until you fill the tin. Freeze for several hours to firm up properly. The freezing between each addition stops the parfait and lemon curd running into one another, so that when you slice it each slab will be spotted with perfect little yellow dots of lemon curd. As the lemon curd melts more quickly than the parfait, as you eat it you will hit little soft pools of it. Quite delicious...

I also like to serve neat lemon curd with ✳ **Crostoli Biscuits** to dip into it. You can buy these from good Italian delis, but they're easy to make. Beat 2 eggs with 60 g sugar, the grated zest of 1 lemon and ½ tablespoon of grappa until the mixture turns white, then stir in 4 tablespoons of warmed milk. Put 300 g sifted plain flour into another bowl, make a well in the centre and pour in the egg mixture, a little at a time, mixing until you have a stiff dough. Add a little more warm milk if necessary. Work in 75 g melted butter, then roll out on a floured surface and cut into strips about 15 cm long and 1 cm wide. Twist the strips, then deep-fry in vegetable oil until golden. Dust with icing sugar when cool.

In Italy I often buy ✳ **Cannoli**, strips of crostoli dough wrapped around wooden dowelling to make little tubes like cannelloni, then deep-fried and, when cool, filled with ricotta mixed with nuts, candied fruit and chocolate chips, or vanilla or chocolate custard.

Classic

Panforte

Still on the classical Italian theme, this is the famous spicy cake from Sienna. It is great to make up in huge batches, then wrap in rice paper with more decorative paper over the top and send to people for Christmas. Wrapped and stored in an airtight container, it keeps for 6–8 months.

Makes one 23-cm cake

115 g whole hazelnuts, coarsely chopped
115 g blanched almonds
40 g dried figs, coarsely chopped
130 g candied orange peel, coarsely
   chopped
130 g candied lemon peel, finely chopped
1 teaspoon grated lemon zest
70 g flour
½ teaspoon ground cinnamon
¼ teaspoon ground coriander
¼ teaspoon ground cloves
¼ teaspoon freshly grated nutmeg
pinch of white pepper
150 g sugar
60 g runny honey
30 g butter
icing sugar, for dusting

1 Preheat the oven to 180°C/350°F/gas 4 and line a loose-bottomed 23-cm cake tin with greased baking paper. Spread the nuts on a baking tray and roast them gently, turning regularly until golden. They will turn from golden to burnt very quickly, so keep an eye on them.
2 Reduce the oven temperature to 150°C/300°F/gas 2.
3 In large mixing bowl, mix the nuts, figs, peel, lemon zest, flour, spices and pepper.
4 In a pan, heat the sugar, honey and butter together and simmer the mixture for about a minute.

5 Pour this syrup into the mixing bowl and stir until thoroughly blended.
6 Pour the mixture into the prepared tin and smooth the top. Work quite quickly, as the mixture will stiffen up rapidly.
7 Bake for 30–40 minutes until the edges are quite firm, but the cake is still quite springy in the centre. It will harden up inside as it cools.
8 Wait until the panforte is completely cool and firm before removing it from the tin, then dust heavily with icing sugar.

Pear Frangipane Tart

The first time I discovered frangipane was a complete revelation. There I was at college, being all arrogant and Australian about anything traditional in cooking, then one day we made frangipane, named after an Italian called Frangipani. Apparently he was living in Paris in the sixteenth century, when he came up with an almond perfume as a scent for gloves – strange, but true. Then, even stranger, the fashionable pastry cooks of the time took this as their inspiration for a new flavour of pastry cream.

Anyway, I mixed up the butter, eggs, flour, sugar and some ground almonds as instructed and couldn't believe how easily they transformed themselves into this gorgeous, puffy, soft sponge, which is one of those clever little miracles in cooking that truly deserves its place on the classic list.

Makes one 23-cm tart

for the poached pears:
3 quite firm pears, peeled
300 ml white wine
100 g caster sugar

1 vanilla pod
1 cinnamon stick
5 blades of mace

for the sweet pastry:
250 g plain flour
90 g caster sugar
zest of ¼ lemon
175 g unsalted butter
1 egg

for the frangipane:
250 g unsalted butter, softened
250 g caster sugar
2 eggs
1 level tablespoon plain flour
250 g ground almonds

1 First poach the pears: put them in a large pan with the wine, sugar, vanilla pod, spices and water to cover. Bring to the boil, then turn the heat down to a simmer and cook for about 10 minutes. Leave to cool in the liquor, then drain.
2 Make the pastry: sift the flour into a bowl and add the sugar and lemon zest. Rub in the butter with your fingertips, until the mixture resembles breadcrumbs. Make a well in the centre and add the beaten egg, working the mixture into a dough. Wrap in cling-film and chill in the fridge for at least half an hour.
3 Roll the pastry out on a floured surface, then use to line a 23-cm tart tin. Put into the fridge again for another half an hour.
4 Preheat the oven to 180°C/350°F/gas 4. Line the pastry case with greaseproof paper, fill with baking beans and bake it blind for 15 minutes. Remove the paper and beans and put back into the oven for another 5 minutes to dry out the base. The pastry should be just starting to colour. Remove from the oven, but leave the oven on.
5 Make the frangipane: cream the softened butter and the sugar together until pale, then slowly beat in the eggs. Beat in the flour and ground almonds until you have a smooth paste. Spoon into the pastry case.
6 Cut the poached pears into halves, remove the cores and arrange the pear halves in a circular pattern on top of the frangipane, pressing in gently.
7 Put the tart into the oven and bake for about 40 minutes, until the frangipane has risen up around the pears and is golden and springy to the touch.

Crème Brûlée There are two schools of thought on this one. Some say *crème brûlée* is classically French, others that it is actually an English creation which used to be known as Cambridge burnt cream until someone decided that this didn't sound smart enough. The other big debating point is how to get the best crunchy *brûlée* topping, which people can smash gleefully. My favourite easy way is to mix some soft demerara sugar and caster sugar, half and half. If you use just caster sugar, you need to keep spraying it with water from an atomizer as you melt it under the grill, or with a blowtorch, to stop it from burning.

However, the really clever way to get a fantastic crunchy topping, if you have the time, is to boil up your caster sugar with a little water until it forms a golden caramel, pour it out on a tray, allow to cool and then put it into the fridge to set. When it is glassy, put it into a food processor and blitz it to crush it into little sand-like grains. Sprinkle that in a

❝ **The other big debating point is how to get the best crunchy *brûlée* topping, which people can smash gleefully** ❞

thin layer on top of your brûlée and, because the sugar has already changed its character during the cooking, it will melt really quickly. When it is set it will be so crunchy that you can actually keep the brûlées, complete with topping, in the fridge for a few hours without the caramel sweating and softening up, as it would do otherwise.

Makes 8

85 g caster sugar
3 whole eggs plus 6 extra egg yolks
850 ml double cream
1 vanilla pod

for the topping:
a little soft brown sugar and caster sugar,
   mixed together in equal quantities

1 Whisk the caster sugar, eggs and egg yolks until pale.
2 Put the cream into a pan with the vanilla pod (split it lengthwise and scrape the seeds into the cream). Bring gently to just below the boil.

3 Remove the vanilla pod and pour the cream slowly over the egg mixture, beating continuously. Return to the pan and cook gently (don't reboil), stirring continuously, until it forms a thick custard. It's really important to scrape the bottom and corners of the pan as it cooks, to stop it curdling, sticking or burning.
4 Pour into ramekin moulds, let cool, then chill for a good couple of hours to set.
5 About 15 minutes before you want to serve, make the topping: preheat a very hot grill and sprinkle the two sugars over the top of the ramekins in a layer about 1 mm thick and put under the grill, or use a blowtorch to melt the sugar.
6 Leave to crisp up before serving.

The other creamy dessert I love (especially with baked rhubarb) is the Italian custard, ✳ **Panna Cotta**, which I can only describe as milky and bosom-like in the best Pre-Raphaelite tradition, with a few vanilla-seed freckles! Bring 600 ml double cream to the boil in a pan with 90 g caster sugar and a vanilla pod, split and the seeds scraped into the cream. When it boils, take it from the heat, stir in 2 gelatine leaves that have been soaked in water, stir until mixed through, then leave to cool, stirring occasionally until it is completely cold. Pour into rounded dariole moulds and leave to set in the fridge overnight. When ready to serve, dip a knife into boiling water and run around the edges of the mould to loosen. Turn the slightly wobbling, silky-smooth custards out on plates.

   Finally, the all-time classic country Australian dessert: ✳ **Pineapple in Jelly**, of which I have fond childhood memories! Take one tin of sliced pineapple rings (I remember the brand was always Golden Circle), one packet of green jelly (it was always Aeroplane Jelly... 'I love Aeroplane Jelly, Aeroplane Jelly for me...'). Take the lid off the can of pineapple, remove the pineapple and drain, but keep the can. Make up the jelly according to the packet instructions. Now for the artistic bit: pour a layer of jelly into the can, let it set, then put in the pineapple rings and pour the rest of the jelly down the centre and over the top. Leave in the fridge overnight. The next day, turn the can upside down and ceremoniously open the other end, slide it off carefully to reveal a little turret of pineapple in green jelly, and serve with vanilla ice-cream!

❛Panna Cotta, which I can only describe as milky and bosom-like in the best Pre-Raphaelite tradition, with a few vanilla-seed freckles!❜

Posh

Posh is as much to do with anticipation and ceremony as the food

For 'posh', read 'sexy'... I'm not talking here about stilted, fiddled-around-with food, or rigid formality, but a bit of the showmanship and excess that we all love from time to time – 'fun posh' where everybody goes home from dinner at your house with a big smile on their face and wakes up the next morning, saying, 'I want another Bloody Mary.'

Posh is as much to do with anticipation and ceremony as the food. It's about extending the leaves of the family table, opening up the drawer where the special cutlery is kept, lighting candles and dressing up, with that wonderful moment of turning to your partner and saying, 'Could you zip me up?' or 'Would you do my cuffs?' It's about plunging a magnum of champagne into the ice bucket, knowing that one of your friends will want to drink lager all night, but that's fine, as long as it's chilled properly and they drink it out of an elegant glass! Good friends don't care about things like that, or whether someone is wearing Versace and everyone else is in jeans, because they know that everyone adds something to the party, whether they make the food, bring an interesting bottle of wine, provide good conversation or just radiate great beauty.

My kind of posh is all bound up with the streak of naughtiness that, at 4.30 on a Tuesday afternoon, makes you take out a packet of water biscuits and a big piece of fantastic cheese and break open a bottle of champagne. Posh can be a table laid with linen, or a rug spread on the grass in the garden, with beautiful glasses and lots of people sharing big bowls of langoustines, halved lengthwise, with lemon wedges and pots of mayonnaise or Aïoli (see page 114), cracking crab claws, or slurping rock oysters bathed in red wine vinegar with shavings of shallots and a little freshly ground white pepper. Or making the poshest sandwiches in the world –

Posh

chunks of lobster between thick slices of good bread with lashings of butter and salt. If you want the really extravagant version, add some sliced tomatoes, a scattering of basil leaves, some good mayonnaise and a little salad of sliced shallots, mixed leaves and flat-leaved parsley, tossed in a mixture of olive oil, a dash of walnut oil, red wine vinegar, Dijon mustard and generous seasoning.

The posh dinner parties I have in mind don't have to be bound by three courses: you can have just one or two great items, or drop little dishes continuously on the table – they can be as simple as you like, perhaps a piece of good bread, such as Poilane sourdough (the famous bread imported from the Paris bakery), toasted, with goats' cheese, scattered with a few leaves and some fantastic olive oil; or scrambled eggs and langoustines; then a piece of grilled fish; a cutlet or two from a rack of lamb crusted with breadcrumbs and herbs; and some fruit and cheese. The luxuriousness comes from the sense of occasion you create and the occasional hint of a hideously expensive ingredient – I love the idea of lavish and more mundane together, like mashed potato and caviare.

I don't believe in rules, but take a little care over your menu, so you don't hit creaminess overload or an uncomfortable clash of ethnic styles: I wouldn't serve a coffee soufflé with chocolate sauce after soy-grilled reef fish or a piece of Japanese marinated tuna, for example, because the saltiness and particular richness of an ingredient like soy sauce would clash with chocolate. European desserts don't generally go with Asian main courses, though you might serve a light Japanese dessert after a European main course. Just try to visualize the flavours and imagine actually eating those combinations before you plunge in and start shopping.

Really I think you could take any recipe from this book, serve it with a bit of panache and make it posh, because you build the atmosphere and set the tone. However, there are also some things that are just impossibly glamorous, like this lobster omelette, drizzled with a rich lobster bisque, thickened in the traditional way with rice that dissolves and reduces down to a rich glaze.

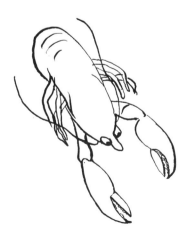

Lobster Omelette This is a hybrid of a crab omelette made by a chef friend of mine, Mike McEnearney, and the traditional Thai rolled omelette that is eaten either plain with curry or filled with pork or greens or seafood, and sold as a snack on the streets. When I first made it, I was looking for something a bit New York or Chelsea, with a touch of decadence, that you could eat for lunch in the sunshine with a bottle of chilled wine and feel quite smart, and I like it because it satisfies that nice notion of mixing glamorous and everyday ingredients.

In Asian supermarkets around Chinese New Year, you can buy bags of snow pea shoots, which are the lovely squiggly tendrils from the tops of pea plants, looking like little butterflies. If you grow peas in your garden, save them and add them to this omelette with the beansprouts. They have a fantastic intense pea flavour that is like sucking on a raw pea pod and that summery aroma that lingers on your hands when you shell fresh peas.

‘There are also some things that are just impossibly glamorous, like this lobster omelette’

Lobster omelette (continued)

2 cooked lobsters, each about 750 g
20 g palm sugar
3 tablespoons fish sauce
12 eggs
350 ml vegetable oil
100 g pea shoots (see page 130), optional
100 g beansprouts
small bunch of garlic chives
handful of Thai basil leaves

for the bisque:
100 ml vegetable oil
2 large onions
3 large carrots
2 celery stalks
6 overripe tomatoes
4 garlic cloves, crushed
100 g rice
2 lemon grass stalks
50 g galangal, chopped
4 whole star anise
100 ml brandy
100 ml fish sauce

to serve:
dash of oyster sauce

1 Take the meat from the bodies of the lobsters and reserve it, together with the claws. Keep the shell from the bodies for the bisque.
2 Make the bisque: heat the vegetable oil in a large heavy-based pot, add the lobster shells and cook gently until they turn dark red.
3 Coarsely chop the onions, carrots, celery and tomatoes, add them to the pot and cook gently for 10 minutes until the vegetables soften. Add the garlic and the rice and cook for 5 minutes, then add the lemon grass, galangal and star anise.
4 Pour in the brandy and bring to the boil, scraping the pan, to get all the bits off the base. Add about 1.5 litres of water and the fish sauce, bring back to the boil, then reduce heat to a simmer and cook for about 2 hours, adding another 500 ml water halfway through cooking time. Remember to stir and scrape the base of the pan regularly so that the rice doesn't stick. By the end of cooking time, the bisque should have reduced to the thickness of a sauce. Strain and keep warm if using immediately. Otherwise, allow it to cool, then keep it in the fridge until you are ready to reheat it.

5 To make the omelette, put the sugar and fish sauce in a pan and heat gently until they form a syrup. Allow to cool.
6 In a bowl, break the yolks of the eggs with a fork, but don't beat the eggs, because you want chunky bits of white and yolk running through the omelette. Add the mixture of fish sauce and palm sugar, and stir gently, trying not to disturb the eggs too much.
7 Put a wok on the hob and warm it, then add half the oil (it is best to make these omelettes in two batches). Heat it until it starts to shimmer, but don't let it smoke, then pour in half the egg mixture, stirring just before it goes in. The eggs will fluff and puff up quite dramatically. Don't disturb them, just leave for about 2 minutes, then flip the omelette over and cook on the other side for another 3 minutes.
8 Lay 2 clean tea towels out flat on your work surface. Drain off the excess oil from the wok, and flip out the omelette on to one of the tea towels.
9 Repeat the process with the rest of the eggs to make a second omelette.
10 Sprinkle some pea shoots (if using), beansprouts, garlic chives and basil leaves (reserving some for garnish) down the centre of each omelette,

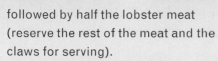

followed by half the lobster meat (reserve the rest of the meat and the claws for serving).

11 Now roll up each omelette, by picking up the end of towel closest to you and drawing it over the top of the omelette, so that it starts to roll up. Use the tea towel to tuck in the edge of the omelette, then continue to roll quite tightly, so that the filling is completely enclosed.

12 To serve: arrange the remaining lobster on a big plate, reserving the 4 claws. Turn the rolled omelettes so that the seam is underneath, trim the ragged ends and cut each omelette in half at an angle. Lay them on top of the lobster meat and drizzle some of the bisque over. Place a lobster claw on top of each omelette half and shake a little oyster sauce around the outside. Garnish with the remaining basil.

Posh

I use the same sauce for a sexy little dish that I have made for years but never tire of, ✳ **Spaghettini with Prawns and Macadamia Nuts**. For a starter for 6 people you need about 600 g spaghettini (thin spaghetti), cooked in plenty of boiling salted water until *al dente*. At the same time, cook 500 g big juicy prawns in plenty of butter (about 100 g) in a big pan, then add a little reduced lobster bisque. Drain the spaghettini and add to the pan of prawns and toss well, so that the sauce clings to the pasta. To make a crunchy contrast with the lusciousness of the sauce and the firm bite of the pasta, sprinkle over 50 g macadamia nuts that have been roasted in the oven for a few minutes until they are golden.

You could also cook the bisque for half the time and serve it as a soup in its own right, perhaps with some chopped lobster meat and sour cream or, to be really extravagant, a single *raviolo* of lobster (see page 136) in the centre of each bowl.

I sometimes make a more simple ✳ **Crab, Spring Onion and Coriander Rolled Omelette**. Instead of adding fish sauce and sugar to the eggs before making the omelette, I add a dash of oyster sauce, then cook the omelette in the same way. For the filling I use 100 g fresh white crab meat, a handful of chopped coriander leaves and a couple of chopped spring onions. The dressing is made with 200 ml dashi, the classic Japanese stock made from dried flakes of bonito (a fish that is related to the tuna) and kombu, or kelp seaweed. You can buy dashi in some better supermarkets. Bring it to the boil in a pan, then turn down the heat to a simmer and add 1 tablespoon of light soy sauce and 1 teaspoon of sake. Cook for a couple of minutes, then drizzle with a squeeze of lime juice over the omelettes.

✳ **Scrambled Eggs with Langoustine Tails** are pretty smart too. For each person you need 3 eggs and 5 langoustine tails, a tablespoon of chopped sweet herbs like basil and parsley, 50 g butter and 3 tablespoons double cream. Beat your eggs in a bowl, then run a knife along the back of the langoustine tails to remove the vein. Melt almost all the butter in a pan and heat the tails through. When they are cooked, add the beaten eggs and cream, and cook slowly, stirring all the time until the eggs are cooked but still soft and creamy. Take off the heat, stir in the remaining butter and herbs, season and serve quickly.

To be really frivolous, you could make ✳ **Scrambled Eggs with Caviare**. For each person, whisk 3 tablespoons crème fraîche to soft peaks and fold in a tablespoon of vodka. Melt a tablespoon of butter in a pan and add 2 beaten eggs and 3 tablespoons double cream. Cook as before, season well, then serve with the crème fraîche spooned on top and a little glistening mound of caviare on top of that.

> **To be really frivolous, you could make Scrambled Eggs with Caviare**

Ravioli

In any restaurant, anywhere in the world, any time, if there is an interesting sounding dish of ravioli on the menu, I have to try it, no matter how tempting the rest of the dishes might be. There is something sensual and slightly mysterious about biting into the beautiful soft, yielding casing and discovering a pocket of flavours that explode in your mouth. I love dumplings for the same reason. The potential for fillings is pretty much unlimited, from intensely rich ones like shredded oxtail, to light summery mixtures such as crab meat, spring onion and ginger. The only rule I would follow is that unwritten Italian one of not combining fish and cheese. I sometimes make round ravioli filled with egg yolks and serve them on top of slightly crunchy asparagus spears, so that when you break into the pasta the egg yolk oozes out.

Pasta Dough

For cannelloni or lasagne, ready-made pasta is fine, but I think that for ravioli you really need to make your own, as home-made pasta is so much more pliable and elastic. The flour must be type '00' (doppio zero), as other flours are too absorbent and won't give you the same stretchiness. Also, probably for the only time in this book, you do need to use table salt, as anything grainier will ruin the texture.

When making pasta dough, just like bread dough, you need to feel your way, adding the eggs a little at a time so that the mixture doesn't get too wet. The quantity you use will probably differ slightly each time you make your pasta, as factors such as humidity and the temperature of the room can play a part.

Makes about 600 g, enough for about 3 good-sized ravioli for 6 people

500 g type '00' flour, plus more for
   dusting
pinch of table salt
4 whole eggs, plus 3 extra egg yolks
1 tablespoon olive oil

1 Put the flour and salt into a food processor, add half the eggs and half the extra yolks and mix until incorporated. Add the oil and process again.

2 Mix the rest of the eggs and extra yolks and start adding this a little at a time, feeling the texture regularly. When ready, it will be like large loose breadcrumbs that will come together as a dough if you squeeze them. You may not need to use all the eggs, or you may even need to add a little more.
3 Tip the mixture out on to a floured surface, push together and knead until it forms a dough.
4 Wrap in cling-film and leave to rest for several hours before use.

> **There is something sensual and slightly mysterious about biting into the beautiful soft, yielding casing and discovering a pocket of flavours that explode in your mouth**

Crab Ravioli with Sorrel

The special thing about this pasta is the way the slightly crunchy, slightly sour-tasting sorrel leaves tossed in olive oil cling to the outside of the ravioli, forming a sort of second skin.

Serves 6 (3 each)

piece of fresh ginger, about 2–3 cm
350 g white crab meat
150 g dark crab meat
2 spring onions, thinly sliced
handful of coriander leaves
pinch of paprika, dry-roasted until aromatic
½ teaspoon salt
600 g pasta dough (see page 135)
flour, for dusting
1 egg, beaten
salt and freshly ground black pepper
3 tablespoons olive oil
handful of baby sorrel leaves

1 Peel and chop the ginger and put it into a food processor or pestle and mortar with 1 teaspoon of water. Pound and crush until it is well broken down, then transfer to a piece of clean muslin and squeeze out the juice into a bowl. Mix with the crab meat, sliced spring onions, coriander leaves, paprika and salt.

2 Put the pasta dough through a pasta machine, according to manufacturer's instructions, or roll it out to about 1 mm thick, working as quickly as you can as the more it dries out the more it will lose its elasticity. If you are rolling it out in batches, keep the remainder moist by wrapping it in cling-film. Cut the dough into 36 circles each about 7 cm in diameter and keep them wrapped in cling-film until you are ready to fill them.

3 Place a little crab mixture in the centre of half the circles, brush the edges with beaten egg, place another pasta circle over the top and pinch well all around the edge to seal.

4 Bring a large pan of heavily salted water to a rolling boil, add a drop of olive oil and put in the ravioli. They will float to the top of the pan and be ready 2 minutes after that (about 4 minutes in all). It is better to cook them in batches in separate pans than cram too many into one pan. Drain well.

5 Meanwhile, pour the remaining olive oil into a large pan and gently warm it through, throw in the sorrel, toss it well in the warm oil and season well with freshly ground black pepper. Take off the heat.

6 Toss the drained ravioli very gently in the oil mixed with the sorrel leaves so that they cling to the outside, and serve.

You could make up the ravioli in the same way, but vary the filling using chopped lobster mixed with rouille (see page 111), or shredded braised oxtail from the recipe that follows. I like to serve oxtail ravioli in duck broth, which you can make using any bones left over from a roast duck. You could use this all-purpose aromatic base for a quick posh soup another time, garnished with whatever you like – perhaps ravioli filled with crab or lobster meat, or dumplings filled with minced prawn or pork – dropped into the broth with some sliced seared scallops, chopped ginger and spring onion (see page 141).

Oxtail Ravioli with Ginger Duck Broth

Serves 6 (2 each)

600 g pasta dough (see page 135)
1 egg, beaten

for the oxtail:
1 kg oxtail, trimmed of excess fat
salt and freshly ground black pepper
a little olive oil
2 carrots, chopped
1 onion, chopped
1 celery stalk, chopped
1 garlic clove, crushed
60 g galangal, chopped
1 whole star anise
200 ml red wine
500 ml beef stock
4 tablespoons dark soy sauce
4 tablespoons fish sauce

for the duck broth:
1 duck carcass or bones left over from
   roast duck (see pages 116–7)
2 tablespoons fish sauce
50 g ginger, sliced
1 lemon grass stalk, outer leaves
   removed and inside chopped
2 whole star anise
handful of coriander roots, chopped
1 tablespoon dark soy sauce
½ teaspoon sesame oil

to serve:
1 large red chilli, deseeded and sliced
2 spring onions, chopped
small bunch of coriander leaves

1 Preheat the oven to 190°C/375°F/gas 5.
2 Season the oxtail well. Heat a little oil in a frying pan, put in the oxtail and fry until well browned on all sides.
3 Heat more oil in a heavy-based pan and add the vegetables, galangal and star anise. Cook briefly until the vegetables are just soft. Add the wine and bubble until the liquid is reduced to a glaze.
4 Add the oxtail, cover with the stock and bring to the boil. Skim the surface, then add the soy and fish sauces.
5 Transfer to the oven and cook for 2–3 hours, or until the meat is very tender.
6 Meanwhile, make the duck broth: put all the ingredients in a pan with 2 litres of water and simmer for about 1 hour.
7 Towards the end of the oxtail cooking time, roll out the pasta dough to about 1 mm thick (see opposite), working as quickly as possible to retain the elasticity. Cut the dough into 24 circles about 10 cm in diameter and wrap in cling-film until you are ready to fill them.
8 Take the meat from the oven and keep warm. Strain the liquid, put it back in the pan and boil up. Keep bubbling until you have a thick sauce. Shred the oxtail and mix with the sauce. Allow to cool.
9 Place a spoonful of oxtail in the centre of half the ravioli rounds, brush the edges with beaten egg and place the remaining ravioli rounds on top. Seal well by pinching around the edges.
10 Bring a large pan of salted water to the boil, add a dash of olive oil, put in half the ravioli and cook for about 4 minutes (they will be done 2 minutes after they float to the surface).
11 Meanwhile, strain the broth into a warmed serving bowl and, when the first batch of ravioli is cooked, keep them warm in it. They will stay nice and plump for about 10 minutes. Quickly cook the rest and transfer to the bowl.
12 Serve garnished with the sliced red chilli, spring onion and coriander.

Wild Mushroom and Goats' Cheese Cannelloni
Serves 6 (2 each)

a little olive oil
300 g mixed wild mushrooms, such as
  chanterelles, ceps, shiitake, etc.
salt and freshly ground black pepper
handful of chopped parsley
10 g butter
1 long shallot, diced
1 garlic clove, chopped
handful of dried ceps

200 ml double cream
6 sheets of ready-made fresh lasagne
300 g goats' cheese, thickly sliced

The day before:
1 Get a pan very hot, add the oil and,
when that is smoking-hot, fry the
mushroom varieties one at a time until
well browned. Season, add the parsley
and set aside.
2 Cook the shallots in the butter until
translucent. Add the garlic and cook for a
few minutes more. Put the dried ceps in a

pepper grinder and use to season.

3 Add the cream and bring to the boil, then bubble until reduced by about two-thirds. Fold in the mushrooms and season again if necessary.

4 While the cream reduces, cook the lasagne in boiling salted water for 2–3 minutes and refresh in cold water.

5 Lay a sheet of cling-film on a work surface, place a sheet of drained pasta on top and arrange one-sixth of the mixture along the length, about 5–6 cm in from the edge. Using the cling-film to help you, roll up into a cylinder, and twist the ends of the cling-film. Repeat with the rest of the pasta and mixture. Chill overnight.

Next day:

6 Preheat the grill to hot.

7 Bring a large pan of salted water to the boil, put in the wrapped cannelloni and cook them for about 5 minutes. Drain well.

8 Snip one end of the cling-film and push out the cannelloni like a sausage. Top each cannelloni with a slice of goats' cheese and put under the grill for a few minutes until the cheese melts, bubbles and browns. Slice each cannelloni in half.

9 Drizzle the cannelloni with olive oil and season with freshly ground black pepper to serve.

You can make ✳**Pumpkin Cannelloni** in a similar way. For the filling cut 200 g gold pumpkin or butternut squash into quarters, then roast with the skin on in the oven at 220°C/425°F/gas 7 for about 20 minutes until the flesh caramelizes (this brings out the flavour) but stays firm. Trim off the skin and mash the flesh roughly with a fork. Melt 50 g butter in a pan, add a chopped shallot and cook until translucent, then add 3 finely chopped garlic cloves and cook for a few minutes more. Add 200 g ricotta cheese and let it melt, then mix in 100 g mascarpone and remove from the heat. Roughly chop 100 g spinach and cook it quickly in a little butter. Stir that into the mixture with the mashed pumpkin and season. Use slices of mozzarella rather than goats' cheese when you put the cannelloni under the grill. Serve with tomato sauce (see page 79) and scatter with some leaves of flat parsley. You can also use the same mixture of pumpkin and cheese as a filling for ravioli.

Chinese Dumplings

There is an elegance about the idea of wrapping one ingredient around a more delicate one to protect it, whether it's rabbit or a piece of sea bass encased in pancetta, a ravioli holding an egg yolk, or a flour-and-water paste rolled thinly and cut into rounds or squares to make a Chinese-style dumpling filled with little morsels of delicately spiced minced pork or prawn.

All these are quite simple to do, but they show you have spent a bit of time and tried to come up with something you wouldn't ordinarily cook. Chinese dumplings are the Eastern equivalent of ravioli and are delightful in just the same way. Steamed, fried or poached, they are traditionally snack food, and take up a big portion of the dim sum trolleys that roll up and down throughout the day in Hong Kong restaurants and the dim sum halls of Chinatown districts around the world.

You can find dumplings ready-filled in Chinese supermarkets, but it is more fun to buy packets of wrappers instead and make up your own fillings. You can serve them in bamboo baskets as starters to be dipped into little bowls of soy sauce spiced with shreds of ginger; or drop them into an aromatic broth and sprinkle them with slivers of spring onions and chilli, crunchy beansprouts and coriander leaves.

Some of the most clever dumplings are ✳ **Pot Stickers**, made in Japan as well as China, which are fried, boiled and steamed all in one go, so that they stay soft on

> **❝ There is an elegance about the idea of wrapping one ingredient around a more delicate one to protect it ❞**

140

top and turn crispy underneath. You use round white wonton wrappers and, for about 20 dumplings, make up a filling with 100 g of finely minced pork, mixed with a tablespoon of very finely chopped spring onion and 1 teaspoon of very finely chopped fresh ginger, 2 teaspoons of light soy sauce, and 1 teaspoon of sesame oil, worked together to form a tight mixture. Put a teaspoonful in the middle of each wonton wrapper, dampen the edges with water, then bring them up and pinch them together, so the dumplings look like little Cornish pasties.

Get a film of vegetable oil hot in a non-stick frying pan and stack the dumplings in tightly, add 2 cupfuls of water, cover the pan and turn up the heat to high. When the water boils, take off the lid and let the liquid bubble and evaporate for 10 minutes, shaking the pan from time to time, until the bottom of the dumplings are crispy and brown, the tops soft and translucent, and the pork inside cooked (you can insert the tip of a knife into one to check).

The dumplings tend to attach themselves to each other, so that they come out in little stacks. Dip them individually into small bowls of soy sauce or a mixture of half light soy sauce and mirin (sweet non-alcoholic Japanese rice wine).

Spiced Duck Soup with Shredded Duck and Oyster Dumplings

This is a pretty sumptuous way of using meat left over from a Chinese roast duck (see pages 116–7). Use the carcass to make the broth (see page 137).

Serves 6

a little roast duck meat, shredded
15 g fresh ginger root, finely chopped
1 garlic clove, finely chopped
1 teaspoon sesame oil
12 oysters
12 square wonton wrappers
2 litres duck broth (see page 137)

to garnish:
2 spring onions, shredded
handful of coriander leaves

1 Mix the duck, ginger and garlic with the sesame oil. Place an oyster in the centre of each wonton wrapper, with a teaspoon of the duck mixture on top. Dampen the edges, gather up like little money bags and seal well.
2 Put the broth into a large pan and bring to the boil. Drop in the dumplings. After a minute or so they will come to the top. Remove from the heat.
3 Serve in warmed bowls, garnished with shredded spring onion and a few whole coriander leaves.

Another variation is ✳ **Duck Broth with Dumplings, Scallops and Ginger**. The dumplings are filled with minced prawn, pork or chicken. Follow the recipe for Pot Stickers above, but steam the dumplings rather than cooking them in oil and water. Sear the scallops in very hot oil in a very hot pan, then slice and add to the bowl of broth and dumplings, with a sprinkling of snow pea shoots (see page 130) and some finely chopped ginger and spring onions.

Posh

Japanese-style Fish
I fell in love over lobster *sashimi*. It was the first time Angie and I ate out together properly, and as I watched her tuck into loads of raw sliced lobster – which seemed quite daring at the time – I thought, 'This has got to be my girl.' There is a lovely purity of flavour and a wonderful ceremony and beauty about Japanese eating which, the first time you experience it, changes your perceptions of food for ever. Fine, delicate presentation is as important as the quality of the ingredients to the Japanese, because in their culture food and artistry are inseparable. It is gorgeous food to have fun with, from finding beautiful crockery to showing off a bit by having a go at carving vegetables.

My definition of posh can be as simple as you like, but it needs an element of the unusual, and if that means straying into new territory, why not? I sometimes think you produce the most exciting dishes when you are completely unrehearsed, and if an idea doesn't turn out quite like you expected, relax – it'll be great next time.

> **There is a lovely purity of flavour and a wonderful ceremony and beauty about Japanese eating**

I love *sushi*. Again it is that experience of something delicate within a wrapper... first comes the punch from the nori seaweed, then the delicate soft taste and texture of the slightly sweet, vinegared rice, followed by a hit of heat from the wasabi (Japanese 'horseradish') and then the wonderful freshness of the filling.

I would buy fish for *sushi* or *sashimi* (slices of raw fish dipped into bowls of soy sauce and mirin) only from a reputable supplier. Otherwise it is hard to be confident that the fish will be as dazzlingly fresh as it needs to be to serve it raw. When you look at a piece of raw fish, if it has a kind of rainbow iridescence, reflecting different colours, then it is not quite as fresh as it should be.

The really exciting stuff is known as *ikejimi*, which is fish caught only by line, never trawled. The idea is to take away the stress of death so the fish dies serenely and you avoid muscle contraction, leaving the flesh tender. As soon as the fish is caught, a thin wire is threaded from the tail through the vertebrae into the brain, puncturing it and switching off messages about decomposition and rigor mortis. The result is fish that is almost completely translucent and not at all stiff.

It is all part of the mystique of Japanese food that *sushi* chefs train for about 10 years to perfect the art of slicing raw fish with razor-sharp knives, finding just the right balance of sweet and sour in the *sushi* rice and creating beautiful little works of art. However, the simplest form of ✳**Sushi Rolls** are quite straightforward to make. You need a bamboo *sushi* mat or a clean tea towel to roll the *sushi*, and some nori sheets (about 18 x 20 cm). The seaweed comes from the shallows around the island of Kyushu in south Japan and is stretched over bamboo frames to dry in sheets, which are then toasted (the sheets may be perforated to make them easier to cut).

For the filling you could use thinly sliced raw tuna, or go for the more modern take on *sushi* which uses ingredients like avocado and crab to make California Rolls, or slices of cooked prawns, or just thin slices of cucumber spread with wasabi.

To make about 24 rolls, you need 4 sheets of nori and 100 g uncooked *sushi* rice (available at good supermarkets). Put the rice into a big pan and cover well with water. Salt it, cover, bring to the boil for 4 minutes, then turn the heat down and leave, covered, for about 20 minutes, until it is cooked but still has a slight crunch. While still warm, fold in 2 tablespoons of mirin mixed with a tablespoonful of rice vinegar, using a wooden spoon. Using chopsticks, fluff up the rice slightly.

Lay a sheet of nori on your mat, shiny side down and perforations running

vertically. Spread the near end with one-quarter of the warm rice and smooth with chopsticks. Lay your filling across the centre of the rice, then smear a strip of wasabi across the remaining rice. Pick up the mat at this end, pull over the top, then push down gently so that the end of the *sushi* roll tucks in and you can use the mat to roll the whole thing up firmly. Tap the ends to neaten, leave to rest for a few minutes, then gently unroll the mat. Slice the roll through the perforations or, if there aren't any, cut it into 3 pieces, then halve these at an angle. Make 3 more rolls and cut each in the same way. Instead of nori, you can use toasted sesame seeds as a coating. Lay a sheet of cling-film on top of your mat, flatten your rice on it and make your roll. Remove the cling-film and roll in sesame seeds before slicing.

There is another clever cheat's way of doing *sushi*. Line a tray with a sheet of nori, cover with a layer of cooked rice, spread it thinly with wasabi, then add a layer of filling, such as crab meat or chopped cooked prawns, then another layer of rice, again spread with wasabi, another layer of crab or prawns, a last layer of rice and finally a top sheet of nori. Cover with cling-film and place something quite heavy, of a similar size, on the top of the tray to weight it down. Put the whole thing in the fridge to chill for about 30 minutes, then remove the weight and top layer of cling-film, turn out and cut the *sushi* into little squares. See if you can find some pickled young ginger as a garnish. It has the most intensely fresh flavour and the pickling process turns the stem a gorgeous shocking pink.

Posh

Sashimi of Tuna with Wakame and Cucumber Salad

Classic *sashimi* consists of slices of raw fish, arranged beautifully, with separate mounds of salad dressed with various combinations of vinegar, mirin, dashi and soy sauce. A little of the dressing is usually served with the *sashimi*, and it will have enough acidity to cook the fish slightly as it is being eaten. The Japanese look for the fatty belly (*toro*) of the blue-fin tuna, but I normally use loin. Wakame is a lobe-leaf seaweed, bought salted or dried. It must be soaked before use, to get rid of the salt or rehydrate it.

Serves 6

70 g fresh wakame, or 20 g dried
1 cucumber
½ teaspoon sea salt (if using dried wakame)
5 tablespoons rice wine vinegar
30 g caster sugar
100 ml light soy sauce
200 g tuna loin

1 Prepare the ingredients several hours ahead. Scrape the salt from the wakame if salted. Peel the cucumber, deseed it and slice it very thinly at an angle. Cover with the salt and leave for 1 hour.
2 Rinse the wakame under cold running water, then leave to soak in cold water for about 5 minutes. Rinse and repeat, then drain and add the vinegar. Leave for another 15 minutes, then drain off the vinegar and keep for the dressing. Tear the wakame into shreds.
3 To make the dressing, put the sugar, soy sauce and the reserved vinegar into a pan, bring to the boil and immediately remove from the heat. Leave to cool.
4 Rinse the salt from the cucumber under cold running water, drain and mix with the wakame. Mix with about half of the dressing and leave in the fridge to marinate for about 3 hours.
5 To serve: using a very sharp knife, slice the tuna very thinly and arrange on a serving plate, with the cucumber and wakame piled up neatly alongside. Serve the dressing in small bowls.

When *sashimi* is hammered until it is very thin and flat it is known as *tataki*. You can do this with salmon or tuna, but I like to make ✳ **Tataki of Sea Bass**, which feels very extravagant because of the expensiveness of the fish. It is served with a dressing of mirin, dashi, sake and two kinds of soy sauce. Incidentally, the Japanese brew the best-quality soy sauce in the world, so whenever you buy any try to make sure it is made in Japan. Even though the Japanese company Kikkoman also brews under licence in other countries, the product is of a different quality.

For 6 people you need 200 g of sea bass fillet. Slice it downwards into 6 thin pieces then lay them, butting up against each other, on separate pieces of cling-film on a work surface. Take 6 more sheets of cling-film and lay them over the top, then hammer the fish until it is wafer-thin. All the slices of fish will join together as you do so. Peel off the top layers of cling-film, then lift the bottom layers and flip over carefully on to a serving plate, so that the fish is transferred without tearing. Peel off the layers of cling-film that are now on top.

Make a salad of 15 g wakame seaweed soaked in water for 10 minutes, drained, then soaked again for another 10, mixed with a few spring onions, sliced thinly at an angle, 10 g chopped pickled ginger, a handful of coriander leaves and about 20 g of enoki mushrooms (trimmed of the ends of their stalks). Make a dressing with 3 tablespoons each dashi (made up according to packet instructions), dark soy sauce, tamari (sweet soy sauce), sake and mirin, sweetened with 50 g sugar. Use a tablespoon or so of this to dress your salad, and pour the rest over the sea bass just before serving. Garnish the plate of fish with a few salmon eggs.

Instead of slicing the fish thinly and serving the salad separately, I sometimes make a ✳ **Tuna Sashimi Salad**, which is a little like a Western tartare, in which the raw tuna is cut into tiny cubes and mixed with the salad ingredients in a dressing of sesame oil, soy sauce, sugar and dashi. For 6 people, first slice 1 peeled and deseeded sweet cucumber, sprinkle with sea salt, then leave for about half an hour. Make a salad with 100 g of shredded Chinese cabbage, 50 g shredded baby spinach, 2–3 spring onions, sliced thinly at an angle, and a small handful of coriander leaves.

For the dressing toast 2 teaspoons of sesame seeds in a dry pan until they begin to colour. Using a pestle and mortar, pound them to a paste with a pinch of caster sugar and a dash of dark soy sauce. Pour 200 ml dashi (mixed according to packet instructions) into a pan and bring to the boil. Then, little by little, mix this into the sesame paste. Leave to cool.

Cut 200 g of raw tuna fillet first into batons about the thickness of chopsticks and then into cubes. Mix these into the salad ingredients and toss in the dressing. Arrange in mounds on your serving plate, with the cucumber, rinsed and tossed with a mixture of 1 tablespoon of rice vinegar and a teaspoon of caster sugar. If you like, you can toast some black sesame seeds in a dry pan until they release their aroma and sprinkle them over the top.

Japanese Glazed Mackerel with Spinach and Sesame Seeds

Simply yet cleverly cooked fish is as much a part of Japanese eating as raw fish. One of my favourite ideas is 'glazing', which involves marinating the fish first, then grilling and basting it until the skin bubbles and turns crisp and the marinade becomes sweet and unctuous.

Serves 6

700 g mackerel fillets, skin on
salt
500 g spinach
50 g sesame seeds
10 g sugar
2 tablespoons dark soy sauce
3 tablespoons dashi (mixed according
   to packet instructions)
1 lemon, sliced, to serve

for the marinade:

2 tablespoons lemon juice

4 tablespoons light soy sauce

4 tablespoons sake

1 Put the fillets in a non-reactive bowl, mix together the marinade ingredients and pour over. Leave for 2 hours, turning the fish halfway through.

2 Bring a pan of salted water to the boil, drop in the spinach and cook for about 1 minute, just enough to wilt it. Drain.

3 Toast the sesame seeds in a dry pan until golden. Using a mortar and pestle, crush with the sugar. Mix well with the soy sauce and dashi until you have a smooth dressing. Add the spinach and work lightly into a solid mass.

4 Divide into 6 pieces and roll each one into a little cylinder. Dip one end into the toasted sesame seeds to coat, then stand the little towers upright on your serving plate, with the ends dusted with sesame seeds facing upwards.

5 Preheat a hot grill and cook the mackerel, skin up, until it blisters and the fish is cooked, basting occasionally with marinade. Cook on this side only.

6 Serve with the spinach and garnish with slices of lemon.

Traditionally Japanese glazed fish is done with oily fish like mackerel, but it also works brilliantly with quite meaty, densely textured white flesh – in Australia we'd use what we call 'reef fish', caught around the Australian reefs, such as red emperor, or make ✳ **Glazed Snapper**. Marinate a 200-g fillet, skin side down, for about 2 hours in a tablespoon of dark soy sauce, mixed with a tablespoon of sake, a dash of mirin and 15 g caster sugar. Just before cooking, turn the fish over. Drain off the marinade and cook under a preheated hot grill, basting frequently, for about 6–8 minutes, until the skin blisters and pops. Then turn it over and finish cooking on the other side.

Serve it with a salad of wakame seaweed, soaked in water for 10 minutes, drained, then soaked again for another 10, mixed with sliced cucumber that has been salted for half an hour, then rinsed and drained. Dress with about 1 tablespoon rice vinegar, 2 teaspoons soy sauce, a pinch of sugar and 10 g grated fresh ginger. Garnish with some shredded spring onion and dry-roasted black sesame seeds.

Prawn Custards make an unusual starter, with an extraordinary texture. For 6 people, peel 200 g prawns, removing the dark vein along the back with a sharp knife. Divide between 6 cocottes. Preheat the oven to 190°C/375°F/gas 5. Mix ½ teaspoon each sea salt and soy sauce with 1 teaspoon sake, 10 g each of shredded ginger and thinly sliced spring onions, and spoon some into each cocotte. Crush a 5-cm piece of peeled, chopped ginger with a teaspoon of water in a food processor or with a mortar and pestle, then squeeze through muslin until you have about a teaspoon of juice. Beat this with 6 eggs, 200 ml dashi (made to packet instructions) and a splash each of light soy sauce and sake. Pour into the cocottes, then put in a roasting pan and pour boiling water in carefully to the same level as the custard. Bake for 20–25 minutes until set, let stand for 10 minutes and serve at room temperature, garnished with chopped coriander.

Posh

Posh Meat

When I was growing up in Australia, veal was so extortionately expensive that it was a really big deal if you were allowed to eat it in a restaurant, and if you had it at someone's house they were either showing off or really rich. Some of the chefs I worked for used to tart up veal in every way they could think of. One, I remember, used to pan-fry veal escalopes, then quarter an avocado and fan it out, put it on top of the veal and smother the whole lot in Hollandaise Sauce and put it under the grill, so that you ended up with a kind of hot avocado cocktail of veal. Even worse was one of the dishes at the restaurant where I got my first job. There the pan-fried veal was doused in a sauce of orange gravy, bacon and mushrooms, covered in Gruyère cheese and again put under the grill.

Despite such attempts to put me off veal for ever, I still think there's something very sumptuous about eating whole roast chunks of it, so much so that I always promised Angie that were we to have a big wedding reception (we didn't) we would serve ✳**Roast Veal**. The best way is to roast a couple of double veal cutlets on the barbie, with some branches of eucalyptus thrown on the coals. First rub the veal well with olive oil, salt and thyme, then roast it slowly for an hour or so, turning it regularly, taking care it doesn't char and the meat doesn't come away from the bones.

At the same time, roast a mass of shallots – the big long ones – in their skins, so that people can pop out the melting insides, and put some big potatoes on the coals. When they're charred on the outside and soft inside, mash them with a little olive oil, lemon juice and salt, and serve with the veal and shallots, a big bowl of olives, a spinach and anchovy salad, and plenty of white wine chilling in buckets of ice. That's the kind of thing I like to do when we throw big summer parties in the garden. We send out proper invitations and lay up long tables and have loads of cold beer and fizz, and the barbecues roaring.

For dinners indoors, I think a ✳**Roast Rack of Lamb** coated in fresh breadcrumbs, with mustard, parsley and garlic, is pretty sexy when you carve it at the table, cutting through the green and gold crust to the tender pink meat inside. For one rack of lamb, seasoned well, you need to mix 100 g fresh white breadcrumbs with 20 g flat parsley, a sprinkling of thyme leaves and a crushed garlic clove, then bind the mixture with 10 g unsalted butter, processing until the mixture is green and quite powdery. Beat an egg with 3 tablespoons of Dijon mustard. Holding the meat by the bones, dip the rack first into the egg and then into the breadcrumb mixture, pressing it in so that it forms a thick coating. Cook in an oven preheated to 190°C/375°F/gas 5 for 12–15 minutes until it is pink, or longer if you prefer your meat more well done. Let it rest for 5–10 minutes in a warm place before carving.

Serve it with Lyonnaise potatoes (sautéed potatoes and onions, sprinkled with parsley) and a salad of baby artichokes, the kind you can buy canned in oil, drained, sliced and mixed with some raw celeriac. Make a dressing by whisking 3 tablespoons of Dijon mustard with a tablespoon of white wine or champagne vinegar, a tablespoon of hazelnut oil, 2 tablespoons of groundnut oil and a pinch of caster sugar, until the mixture is dull with no globules of fat on the surface. Then fold in 210 ml of single cream and toss through the vegetables.

> **The best way of all is to roast a couple of double veal cutlets on the barbie, with some branches of eucalyptus thrown on the coals**

Rabbit with Pancetta Ask your butcher to joint a rabbit for you, leaving you with the baron (saddle, or whole loin, boned, and legs), liver and kidneys. Ask for the legs to be taken off but keep them, as they can be used for confit (see page 88) or, if boned, you could stuff them with a herb butter and roast them.

For 4 legs you need about 170 g unsalted butter, beaten until it is white, mixed with a tablespoon each of chopped tarragon and chopped parsley and a little less of chopped sage, and seasoned. Open out the rabbit legs and spoon the mixture inside, then pull the flesh together to enclose this stuffing and wrap tightly in pancetta. Leave in the fridge for half an hour to firm up, then roast in an oven preheated to 200°C/400°F/gas 6 for 15–20 minutes. To serve, slice each leg in half, pour the pan juices over the top and garnish with a bunch of watercress.

The idea of wrapping rabbit with either pancetta or prosciutto is that they protect the flesh and add a saltiness. I prefer pancetta because it is more smoky and, as it is so thin and streaked with lard, it looks very attractive – but it is up to you. Serve the rabbit with a big bowl of Champ (see page 80), which I reckon can be every bit as posh on the right occasion as it is comforting on others.

Serves 2

8 slices of pancetta or prosciutto
1 boned loin of rabbit with liver and kidneys
freshly ground black pepper
1 tablespoon olive oil

1 Preheat the oven to 200°C/400°F/gas 6.
2 Lay the slices of pancetta or prosciutto on a large piece of foil so that they overlap each other slightly. Open out the loin of rabbit on a clean work surface. Cut the rabbit liver and kidneys in half and lay them down the centre of the rabbit. Season with black pepper – no salt, because the pancetta or prosciutto adds the salt. Bring the sides of the rabbit up to enclose the liver and kidneys and place it across the strips of pancetta or prosciutto. Use the foil to roll up the rabbit in the pancetta, making sure it is completely enclosed, and twist the ends of the foil.
3 Heat the oil in a heavy-based pan, put in the foil parcel and cook for about 2 minutes, then turn over and cook for about 5 minutes more.
4 Transfer the parcels to the oven and cook there for about 15 minutes. Remove from the oven and allow to rest for a good 5 minutes.
5 With a sharp knife, carve it into slices through the foil. Discard the foil and serve. The meat will be just cooked and the offal slightly pink.

Talkin' Pigeon Pigeon roasted as in the recipe opposite always makes a good posh dish and once you have some roast pigeon you can put together several impressive little treats. The breasts of a couple of roasted pigeons make a distinctive ✳ **Pigeon and Beetroot Salad** for a starter with 200 g beetroot cooked in its skin in enough salted water to cover until just tender and left to cool in its own liquor. When it is cool, peel it and cut into small wedges. Bring about 50 g redcurrant jelly and 4 teaspoons malt vinegar to the boil in a large pan, and then let this bubble until the mixture is reduced by half. Put in the beetroot and stir well to coat it. Season, then take the pan from the heat and leave to cool.

Make a dressing with 3 tablespoons of olive oil, a teaspoon of Dijon mustard, a teaspoon of red wine vinegar and a squeeze of lemon juice and season well. Toss some endives in a little of this dressing and pile up on plates, with some beetroot on top and then the pigeon. Pour over a little more of the dressing, scatter with chopped chives and finish off with a good grinding of black pepper.

In season, you could make another lovely fresh salad with the roasted pigeon and some fresh baby broad beans or soya beans, tossed in a similar dressing. Another unusual way to serve pigeon is ✳ **Red-cooked Pigeon with Prickly Ash**. Bring 2 litres of water to the boil with 200 ml Chinese Shaoxing wine, 100 ml light soy sauce and 3 tablespoons dark soy sauce, 100 g yellow rock sugar, 50 g chopped dry-roasted cassia bark, 100 g chopped ginger, 1 chopped garlic clove and 1 chopped spring onion. Fill the cavities of 4 pigeons with 1 teaspooon five-spice powder, roasted in a dry pan with 4 star anise, 1 chopped spring onion and a teaspooon each of salt and sugar. Secure with a skewer. Put in the pan and simmer for 5 minutes, take off the heat and leave the pigeons to steep until the liquid is at room temperature.

Take the birds from the stock, drain the cavity juices and reserve. Leave the birds to get cold in a cool place, pat dry and deep-fry, then break into pieces – which will be a dramatic dark red. Toast 10 g Szechwan peppercorns in a dry pan until they pop, release their aroma and colour slightly, then blitz in a food processor with 90 g salt. Sprinkle over the crispy pigeon and serve with lemon wedges and the reserved juices.

Pigeon, Cabbage and Ceps

Unlike most game, pigeon is hung only briefly, otherwise the bird takes on a sour taste. If you can, buy pigeons that have been grain-fed; they are more expensive but really good quality.

I love this pigeon with slightly crunchy cabbage and the smoky flavours of bacon and dried ceps, which go straight into the pan without being soaked first.

a little olive oil
salt and freshly ground black pepper
4 pigeons
100 g smoked bacon or pancetta,
  cut into pieces
about 20 dried ceps
1 cabbage, cut into chunks
squeeze of lemon juice

1 Preheat the oven to 220C°/425F°/gas 7.
2 Heat the oil in a big ovenproof pan. Season the pigeons, put them into the pan and cook until browned, then remove and keep warm.
3 Add a little more oil to the pan and, when hot, add the bacon or pancetta, dried ceps and cabbage. Toss them around until they colour.
4 Put the pigeons back in the pan on top of the bacon, ceps and cabbage, cover and cook in the oven for about 10 minutes, until the meat is pink but the leg meat comes easily from the bone.
5 Squeeze lemon juice over to serve.

Posh

Desserts Since I don't have a rampant sweet tooth, producing any pudding at home shows I am making an effort, but I guess for most people a posh dessert is one that has either a little more finesse than usual or a load of decadence. I think all of these meet one or other of the criteria...

Caramelized Pear Tart Fine

Serves 6

250 g caster sugar
6 pears, peeled, halved and cored
2 tablespoons Poire William liqueur
300 g puff pastry

1 Put the sugar into a pan with 3 tablespoons water and cook until you have a golden caramel.
2 Add the pears and liqueur, and cook gently, basting the pears with caramel, for 5 minutes. Remove from the heat and leave the pears to cool in the caramel.
3 Meanwhile, preheat the oven to 200°C/400°F/gas 6 and cut out six 10-cm pastry circles. Prick centres with a fork.
4 The pears firm as they cool, so you can slice them. Arrange on the pastry bases.
5 Bake for 8–10 minutes, until the pastry is golden and pears have caramelized.

Blueberry Mascarpone Tart

Makes one deep 23-cm tart

375 g mascarpone, plus more to serve
4 eggs
250 g caster sugar
100 ml Kirsch or berry eau-de-vie, plus more to serve
200 g ground almonds
50 g flaked almonds
150 g blueberries, plus more to serve

for the sweet pastry:
250 g plain flour
90 g caster sugar
zest of ¼ lemon
175 g unsalted butter
1 egg

1 First make the pastry: sift the flour into a bowl and add the sugar and lemon zest. Rub in the butter with your fingertips until the mixture resembles breadcrumbs. Make a well in the centre and add the beaten egg. Work the mixture into a dough. Wrap in cling-film and chill for at least half an hour.
2 Roll out on a floured surface and use to line a 23-cm tart tin. Chill for 30 minutes.
3 Preheat the oven to 200°C/400°F/gas 6. Line the pastry case with greaseproof paper, fill with baking beans and bake blind for 10 minutes. Remove the paper and beans and put the tart back in the oven for another 5 minutes to dry out the base. The pastry should be just starting to colour. Turn the oven down to 150°/300°F/gas 2.
4 Beat the mascarpone with the eggs and sugar. Add the Kirsch or eau-de-vie and the ground and flaked almonds. Spoon half the mixture into the tart case, sprinkle the blueberries over the top and cover with the remaining mixture.
5 Bake for 40–50 minutes until the filling is just firm. Leave to cool.
6 Serve with a bowl of blueberries and an extra bowl of mascarpone, flavoured with the Kirsch or eau-de-vie.

Chocolate Tart

You can't get much more sumptuous than melt-in-the-mouth chocolate. Buy the best you can, at least 70 per cent cocoa solids.

Makes one 23-cm tart

2 eggs, plus 2 extra yolks
50 g caster sugar
250 g dark chocolate
150 g unsalted butter
one 23-cm sweet pastry case, baked
   blind, as opposite.

1 Preheat the oven to 180°C/350°F/gas 4.
2 Beat the eggs and egg yolks with the sugar until the mixture is pale.
3 In a heatproof bowl set over a pan of barely simmering water, melt the chocolate with the butter. Remove from the heat and stir into the egg mixture.
4 Pour into the pastry case and bake in the preheated oven for about 35 minutes, until the surface feels firm to the touch.
5 Leave the tart to cool completely before serving.

Chocolate Cake with Ganache is pretty serious stuff. For a 23-cm cake, put 50 g cocoa powder, 125 g unsalted butter and 125 ml vegetable oil in a pan with 250 ml water. Bring to the boil, then take off the heat. Preheat the oven to 180°C/350°F/gas 4. Break 125 g dark chocolate (at least 70 per cent cocoa solids) into small pieces and put in a large bowl with 375 g caster sugar. Slowly add the cocoa mixture, whisking until the chocolate dissolves and the mixture is cool. Beat in 2 eggs and then sift in 250 g plain flour with 15 g baking powder and gradually fold in. Stir in 125 ml buttermilk, pour into a greased and floured cake tin and bake for 1–1½ hours, until the top is springy and a skewer put into the centre comes out clean. Let cool on a wire tray while making the filling. Break up 300 g dark chocolate into a bowl. Bring 225 ml double cream to the boil, pour it over the chocolate, beating until it melts, then fold in 375 ml single cream. Slice the cake in half, sandwich with half the filling and spread the rest on top. The final luxurious coating of ganache is made by breaking another 200 g of dark chocolate into a bowl, bringing 150 ml double cream to the boil in a pan with 75 ml each of golden syrup and vegetable oil, then pouring this over the chocolate and stirring until it is melted. Smother the cake in the ganache and leave it to cool.

Coffee Soufflé

I prefer to whisk egg whites by hand, as machines tend to over-aerate them. Machine-beaten egg whites look beautifully fluffed up, but left for a minute they will drop and you get liquid in the bottom, as friction has destroyed their structure. Whisking by hand gives you less dramatic – but more even – bubbles. You need to whisk quite hard, though; if your arm gets tired, whisk in short, firm bursts. The egg whites are ready when as frothy as the top of a cappuccino.

Add the sugar little by little. After sprinkling in the first batch, wait until your whisk leaves ribbon-like trails before adding a little more, and so on, until you have a silky meringue with a lovely sheen. It should be firm enough to hold the bowl safely upside down over your head!

Makes 10

a little softened butter for the dishes
4 tablespoons caster sugar,
    plus more for the dishes
2 tablespoons instant coffee powder or
    granules
whites of 7 eggs and yolks of 3 (if you
    like, you can use the remaining yolks
    for Hollandaise Sauce, see pages
    103–4, or custard, see page 97)

for the Chocolate Sauce:
200 g dark chocolate
3 tablespoons double cream

1 Preheat the oven to 200°C/400°F/gas 6. Brush 10 individual soufflé dishes or large ramekins with a little melted butter, then sprinkle in some caster sugar and shake and turn the dishes until the sugar coats the melted butter. Tap out any excess.
2 Put the coffee powder and sugar in a pan with about a teaspoon of water and bring to the boil, stirring to dissolve the coffee and sugar. Remove from the heat and leave to cool.
3 When the mixture is cool, beat in the egg yolks.

4 Whisk the egg whites until they form frothy peaks, then slowly and gently add your sugar a little at a time until the mixture is firm and shiny.
5 Very gently fold about a quarter of the coffee mixture into the egg whites, trying to keep as much air in as possible. It is best to use the whisk or your hand, so you can really feel the texture. Then fold in the rest of the coffee mixture in the same way.
6 Fill the soufflé dishes up to the top, then run your thumb around the inside of the rim to help ensure that the soufflés don't catch and stick as they try to rise (it is only the top half of the soufflé which expands and rises, the base cooks *in situ*).
7 Put the dishes in the oven and cook for 8 minutes or until they are golden and well risen, but still wobble slightly when shaken gently.
8 When the soufflés are almost ready, make the Chocolate Sauce: put the chocolate and cream into a pan, bring to the boil, then remove from the heat and stir well to combine.
9 At the table, break into the top of each soufflé with the tip of a spoon and pour in a little of the chocolate sauce.

Armagnac Prunes

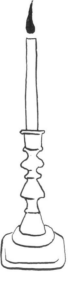

2 tea bags, preferably Earl Grey
250 g pitted prunes
125 g caster sugar
1 cinnamon stick
3 strips of orange peel
2 strips of lemon peel
150 ml Armagnac

1 Bring 600 ml water to the boil in a large pan, add the tea bags and stir around to make a weak tea.

2 Add the rest of the ingredients except the Armagnac and bring back to the boil, then turn the heat down to a simmer and cook the prunes gently for 30–40 minutes. Turn off the heat and leave to cool.

3 When the pan contents are cold, stir in the Armagnac and eat immediately, or transfer to sterilized jars, seal and keep in the fridge for up to a month.

Australian Petits Fours If I'm feeling a bit posh when friends come for dinner, I serve chunks of very bitter chocolate with coffee. There is something wonderfully indulgent about putting the coffee pot on the table, popping the stopper on a decanter of brandy, and passing around plates of small and wicked confections. They don't need to be elaborate *petits fours*.

If ever I needed proof that most food can be smart if you serve it with a bit of style, it was underlined for me at the restaurant Jean Georges in New York. The amazing Jean-Georges Vongerichten prepared lunch of eleven courses accompanied by nine different wines, with a gorgeous soufflé to finish. When coffee arrived, the waiter appeared carrying a massive jar, saying, 'Gentlemen, it's time for marshmallows.' The jar's contents were amazingly delicious tiny home-made sweets, flavoured with chicory, caramel and vanilla.

On one occasion, for a bit of fun at the end of a meal, I made up some plates of a selection of confections that would normally be more at home at a kids' party: honeycomb; my version of Rolos, with toffee moulded into sausage shapes, put into the freezer to harden, then coated in chocolate and sliced; some marshmallows I bought from a good confectioner, rolled in coconut that had been toasted in a dry pan; and a couple of things that any Australian would immediately recognize – rocky road and Lamingtons.

As kids we used to pile into the local chocolate-maker, called Daryl Lee, to buy massive bits of liquorice, chocolate koalas and frogs and, around Christmas-time, tiny boxed Christmas puddings made out of nougat and something fudgy. The sweet we loved most, though, was ❊**Rocky Road** – big slabs of chocolate with marshmallows and nuts. We'd go in and order it by the kilo. Nowadays I make mine by mixing up whole Brazil nuts, whole marshmallows and dark chocolate, then spooning the mixture into a terrine mould or a bread tin that has been lined with baking paper and leaving it to set, out of the fridge, before breaking it into fairly small chunks.

Mention the word ❊**Lamingtons** to most Australians and it will bring a smile to their faces. I have no idea where the name comes from, but these are the home-made treats that every Australian Brownie or Boy Scout or schoolchild has sold at some time on doorsteps – along with snowballs and meringue nests – to raise money for various good causes. You make, or buy, a Genoese sponge, cut it into big cubes, then make up a chocolate sauce by putting 250 g icing sugar, 25g cocoa powder, 2 tablespoons of boiling water and a knob of butter into a pan, and bringing the lot to the boil. Let it bubble away for 3–4 minutes, then take it off the heat. Have ready a plate of desiccated coconut and dip your cubes of sponge cake first in the warm chocolate sauce, then into the plate of coconut until they are coated all over, and then leave to cool.

Serve an assortment of all these goodies on some very smart plates, together with good hot, strong coffee and a selection of liqueurs, and that is about as posh as an Australian gets! But I guess for me that sums up what food should always be about – having fun!

Index

Acknowledgments

Extremely special thanks to 'her ladyship' Sheila Keating for her undivided attention, painstaking translations, unwavering patience and constant hangovers; she has made this the very special book that it deserves to be.

I would also like to thank Tim and Liam for allowing Sheila to give up so much time away from her family to get the book done.

A big 'thank you' to everyone at Quadrille, especially Anne Furniss, who was game enough to commission a book that made perfect sense to us, but had to be translated on to the page. Thanks also to designer Lawrence Morton, who dived in at the deep end with a glorious mix of originality, naïvety and disregard for rules; and to Art Director Mary Evans, who only reined him in ever so slightly. To photographer David Loftus, one man – and his family – on a boat; big hugs and kisses, you're brilliant, mate! And to project editor Lewis Esson, who, beyond his patience and professionalism, has that rare quality of being a good listener.

In the restaurant business we all learn – and 'lift' recipes – from each other, so thanks to all the people I have worked with, whether they have loved or hated me, or aren't quite sure. Beyond that, there's no need for lists of names, because the people who are important in my life know who they are....

John Torode